C000088111

A WALKERS' GUIDE TO NORFOLK

John Pardy

a
CASTELL
publication

RICHARD CASTELL PUBLISHING LIMITED

A WALKERS' GUIDE TO NORFOLK
COPYRIGHT © 1997 RICHARD CASTELL PUBLISHING LIMITED

ISBN 0 948134 41 0

First Published May 1997 by
RICHARD CASTELL PUBLISHING LIMITED
Thwaite, Eye, Suffolk IP23 7EE.

Text © 1997 John Pardy

Printed by
THE GIPPING PRESS
Lion Barn Industrial Estate, Needham Market, Suffolk IP6 8NZ

CONTENTS

Upton Dyke (Walk 15)

INTRODUCTION

ANYONE EXPLORING NORFOLK will soon become aware of the rich diversity of a county where rolling pastures give way to clear slow-flowing rivers, and vast open expanses lead to fenland interspersed with dykes and cuts. A coast exposed to the full force of easterly winds turns, in the north, to wild marsh-bordered land protected in some degree by spits of sand and shingle alive with the sound of birds.

It is this diversity which I have attempted to portray in the 25 walks described in this book which covers a wide area from Lynn and Weybourne in the north to Thetford Forest and Loddon in the south. Norfolk is an excellent area for walking with over 3,000 miles of footpaths and bridleways. The book aims to bring the area and its scenery to life by including more than just the directions for each walk. Each walk has been chosen for its own interest and charm either because of its proximity to particularly beautiful countryside, the history associated with the immediate area or the interest inherent in the village or market town included in the walk.

The first part of the book includes a general introduction to the county together with a section on the development of the landscape, its geology and history and how this resulted in the modern Norfolk we see today.

The bare bones of the route details of each walk are filled out with information of the sort usually found in nature trail leaflets; descriptions of birds and plants likely to be seen during the walk are included along with details regarding scenery and local history, and there are brief notes on some of the churches and other historical buildings encountered on the way. I have intertwined these notes at the points at which they arise on the ground but as they are in a different typeface they can be ignored by those who do not share my enthusiasms. However, I hope they will arouse or develop an interest in the surroundings.

Each walk is circular in route thus avoiding the need for return journeys along the outward path, or wearisome transport arrangements to return to the start point. All the walks were first researched from local O.S. maps to find paths and lanes which provided a circular route without too much use of busy roads.

Initial details of each walk include a map reference of the start point, parking suggestion and the distance and time needed for each walk. The latter is fairly generous but does not allow for long stops for lunch, wandering around villages, or bird watching etc. Places for refreshment are included if convenient at the half-way stage or end of the walk. (A packed lunch is suggested if none are available. Generally I have relied on the latter and so cannot pass comment on the inns mentioned!)

Many of the walks are admirably signed or waymarked either by Norfolk County Council or by a local organisation such as the Broads Authority. Only a few are poorly signed. However, I have included detailed directions for all the walks. It may be thought that some of these are unnecessary but they are included to give confidence to those for whom an open space or a field with no stile in sight can be forbidding. All the landowners and farmworkers I have met have been only too helpful and an 'Oh, am I on the wrong path?' has always elicited a friendly re-direction when necessary.

However, signs can sometimes fall to the ravages of the weather, crops can necessitate detours or a way be blocked by undergrowth or the lush growth of summer and the ubiquitous nettle! Therefore it is useful, although not essential, to have the appropriate O.S. Landranger map to help with an alternative route if necessary. Even here, though, not all the red dotted lines on existing publications remain as rights of way today and in some cases 'concessionary' paths have taken their place.

Whilst Norfolk rarely has the extremes of weather experienced in some parts of Great Britain certain things should be borne in mind regarding suitable clothing. High winds can be frequent especially in winter and low rainfall does not mean that ground cannot still become very muddy. Good walking boots or stout shoes are advisable to cope with frozen ploughed soil, the mud of fields and riverside paths or the hard rutted tracks of summer. The wind chill factor is something to be considered and also the lower temperature often experienced near river or coastal walks.

Details of the Countryside Code are given on page 42. Please do all you can to preserve plant and animal life and to avoid causing problems for all those for whom the countryside is a workplace.

In my own research for this book I have used a number of useful sources so a bibliography is included, as is space for personal notes on the walks.

Map Reading. A map reference is given for the beginning of each walk. The first two numbers of the six figures refer to the number at the top or bottom of the map and the fourth and fifth numbers to those at the sides of the map. For the third and sixth numbers imagine that each square of the map is subdivided into a hundred smaller squares i.e. 10 by 10. If the third and sixth of the reference were 5 that would indicate a point in the middle of the square. Other examples are given on page 118 using an example of a map. Maps needed to cover all the walks in the book are Landranger Nos. 134, 133, 132, 144 and 143, although the last only covers two of the walks.

INTO NORFOLK

TO A STRANGER Norfolk can be an intriguing county which on exploration turns out to be far from the dull featureless area it may appear on the surface. The modern traveller can approach Norfolk from a variety of directions but quite likely it will be along either the A17, the A1065, the A140 or the A12. If a group of four people were to take one of these routes each and arrange to meet in the centre of the county to compare notes they would have very different stories to tell. One might report on dull, apparently featureless character of the north-west but would be full of the beauty and wildness of the north coast between Hunstanton and Sheringham. Another would tell of endless forest and flat countryside relieved only by sizeable market towns that still retained some of their Georgian charm despite their encircling light industries. The third, especially if he took the occasional side road, would describe compact villages which revealed their ancient history through medieval farm and house. The last, as he turned inland beside the River Bure, would describe the watery landscape of marsh and broad interspersed with picturesque villages and fertile land.

Norfolk is indeed a county showing great variety. With an area of 2,073 square miles it is one of wide open spaces - less than five per cent is built up - and, despite being the fourth largest county after Yorkshire, Lincolnshire and Devon, it ranks twentythird in size of population. Although flat - the highest spot is only 346 ft above sea level and parts of the Fens are a few feet below - it is by no means dull. Unlike many counties with obvious features such as the rolling downs of Berkshire and Wiltshire or the fells of Cumbria, Norfolk reveals hidden qualities. It is a county of villages, farms, the occasional small town and, as Hadfield remarks in his book, 'one wide awake city.' Well over half the population live in villages with less than 600 people. It is a county with extensive views and huge skies with always a church tower on the horizon or just round the corner. It is a county renowned for its long, ninety mile coastline stretching from Lynn to Great Yarmouth which is summed up so well by Peter Sager in his book on East Anglia: 'What a coast this is, with its salt marshes and lavender, the channels, dunes, bays and crumbling Ice Age cliffs, lonelier and wilder than its Suffolk neighbour, Arctic, melancholic, beautiful, treacherous, with sandbanks and quicksands, storms and floods and never ending erosion.'

The county is in one sense a cul-de-sac - one does not go through the county to reach another part of England - and this has helped to preserve its unspoilt nature. It has never figured largely in the country's times of unrest and war, until 1940 with the construction of wartime airfields. Numerous castles were not needed to subjugate the population in Norman times; the Wars of the Roses did not intrude, and although families were divided and there was wide support for the Parliamentarian cause, Civil War battles were fought elsewhere. Although some market towns were favoured by the Georgians, they and the Victorians considered beauty could only be found in the Lakes and the Highlands and so, until the railways, passed the county by.

Norfolk's comparative isolation has perhaps helped to form the spirit of its people. From Boadicca, Hereward, Kett, through to the emigrants on the Mayflower, and those seeking a new life in times of agricultural depression, fearlessness and independence have been chracteristics of the 'north folk.'

Map A: Norfolk showing the rivers & main towns.

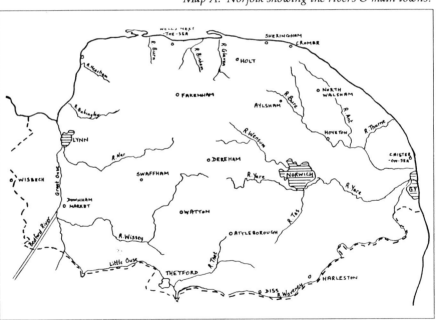

GEOLOGY AND THE LANDSCAPE

THE MODERN LANDSCAPE of Norfolk has evolved naturally over millions of years and man has played a significant part in this only in the last forty thousand years. To appreciate our twentieth century landscape it is necessary first to look back those millions of years to show how it was laid down and later transformed and then to see how the combination of weather, erosion and man's efforts have altered the countryside in more recent times. Some knowledge of the geology of the area will, therefore, be helpful.

The immense time scale of geological history is extremely difficult to appreciate. Only a tenth of geological time is concerned with the period following the Pre-Cambrian era, a time when some of the rocks in N.W.Scotland and Anglesey, for instance, were laid down. (See the Geological time chart on page 10). There followed a period of mountain building, the depositing of limestones and later, in a sub-tropical climate, the growth of vegetation which was the basis later for coal seams. A further period of mountain building and the formation of sandstones ended in the drowning of most of England by seas and the formation of chalk beds over large areas of Britain. Further erosion and volcanic activity was followed by an uplift when our island began to achieve the shape it is today. The land mass shelved eastward and south east England was periodically submerged by seas.

Compared with many areas of the British Isles Norfolk, like the rest of East Anglia, is the baby in geological terms. Although the county is underlain by Pre-Cambrian rocks similar to what can be readily seen in areas of Wales or Scotland (in Norfolk these are at depths of 200 metres in the South West of the county and, considerably deeper - down to a thousand metres - in the North East) the surface rock was laid down much later during the Upper Cretaceous period. Then a bedrock of chalk was deposited about one hundred and forty million years ago. This took place over an immensely long period of time. Geologists have estimated that the minimum time in which 1 metre of chalk could be formed was 83,330 years or approximately 12 metres in a million years. The thickness of chalk underlying Norfolk would therefore have taken over 32 million years to be deposited.

In Norfolk the chalk reaches the maximum thickness of very nearly 400 metres. Much of southern England was covered by sea and it was the hard particles of minute floating plants called coccoliths and other planktonic creatures which formed the chalk and which contribute to its fine grain

THE GEOLOGICAL TIME CHART

Millions of years ago	Begins Period	Era	Events
1.8	Quaternary		Anglian ice sheet. Period of glaciations
5	Pliocene		
22.5	Miocene	Cenezoic	
38	Oligocene Tertiary		Alps and Himalayas formed.
54	Eocene		
65	Palaeocene		
			Chalk deposits formed. Evolution of flowering plants.
141	Cretaceous		
195	Jurassic	Mesozoic	
230	Triassic		Dinosaurs dominant
280	Permian		Coal seams laid down.
345	Carboniferous		
395	Devonian	Palaeozoic	
435	Silurian		
500	Ordovician		Volcanic activity in Wales & Lakes.
570	Cambrian		
2500	Pre-Cambrian		Pre-history of Scotland.

consistency. The lower bands of chalk are greyer and harder and do not contain any nodules of flint which are common in the upper bands of white softer chalk. The flint concentrations of pure silica - formed from sponges and other tiny marine creatures - occur in layers or bands of nodules which formed as the chalk was laid down. They were to become a major building and decorative material for many churches and cottages in East Anglia.

In succeeding millennia other sedimentary deposits were formed including the West Walton beds and the soft, red Kimmeridge clay which surfaces near Hunstanton. Sands were laid down and some became cemented by iron oxide, as in the cliffs at Hunstanton, to form sandstone or carrstone, later to be used in the building of several local churches (see Walk 21). Horizontally striped layers of carrstone and chalk ranging in colour from ginger to white form the sixty foot high cliffs at Hunstanton. Earth movements caused these cretaceous beds to tilt and slope from west to east, so whilst at Hunstanton the chalk is at the top of the cliff, at Weybourne it is at the foot. Further east at Great Yarmouth, it lies several hundred feet below sea level.

The Quaternary period was a time when the climate took over and there was a sequence of cold and warm periods. The history of the glaciations at this time is uncertain as one glaciation could remove the evidence of another. There was certainly a succession of glacial advances and recessions which moulded the landscape which we see in Norfolk today. It is thought that two early glaciations about 1½ million years ago were followed by a warmer period called the Cromer interglacial (because of deposits which now form the cliffs between Cromer and West Runton.) The Anglian glaciation then occurred about 270,000 years ago and reached the north-east coast of Norfolk bringing with it erratics from Oslo and depositing the boulder clays of Cromer till. A temperate period followed known as the Hoxne Interglacial and some human habitation occurred at this time (see page 21).

Ice returned, the Wolsonian glaciation, to last for about 50,000 years. This time glacial action only reached the area of the Wash and the west of the county, but nevertheless the whole of Norfolk would have been subject to

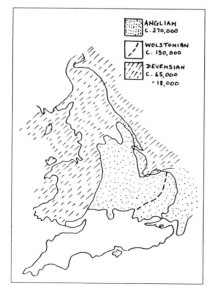

ANGLIAN
C. 270,000

WOLSTONIAN
C. 150,000

DEVENSIAN
C. 65,000
- 18,000

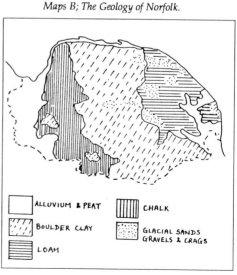

Maps B; The Geology of Norfolk.

ALLUVIUM & PEAT

BOULDER CLAY

LOAM

CHALK

GLACIAL SANDS
GRAVELS & CRAGS

11

permafrost. A warmer period intervened - the Ipswichian interglacial when higher temperatures encouraged animals like rhinoceros and hippopotamus to live here. This, in turn, was succeeded by yet another glaciation, the Devensian about 65,000 years ago. Whilst this affected large areas of the north and west of the country, in the east it only came as far south as the north coast of Norfolk, throwing up the Cromer ridge.

These successive glaciations and intervening periods of warmth brought with them the rich glacial till - boulder clays and sediments - that has made Norfolk such a rich, agricultural county. Glaciations, which in Scotland and other mountainous areas helped to create the corries, hanging valleys and moraine dammed lakes, in Norfolk deposited the rich soils that determined the county's agricultural future.

It is thought that the final ice sheet retreated from the area 10,000 years ago. About 6,500 years ago with the warmer climate, the melting glaciers and the rising sea level drowned the land bridge to the continent and Britain became an island.

Both from a geological and historical point of view Norfolk can be divided into nine regions each of which has its own character and distinctive image. The regions are:
High Norfolk, the Broads and North Coast, the North East, Good Sands, the Chalk Scarp, West Lowlands, Marshland, the Fens, and Breckland (see map). Their individual nature derives partly from man's activities over the centuries although the landscape man found did dictate the use to which it could be put. The character of three of the areas particularly, the Broads, the Fens and Breckland, have, as will be seen in the next chapter, been considerably changed by past generations.

High Norfolk, or central Norfolk, is an upper chalk area noted for its rich boulder clays giving a medium to heavy soil. The central area averages between 150-250 feet above sea level and is characterised by a long eastern slope with wide, deep valleys and wooded uplands. It is crossed by the Rivers Yare and Wensum. In the south the land is lower and the soil heavier. Although rarely rising above 150 feet the River Tas has its source here. There are more villages and less woodland.

Broadland and the North Coast are areas of marshy alluvium soils. The Broads, including the Isle of Flegg - parts of which are below sea level - covers an area of over 200 square miles and has 180 miles of navigable rivers. There are numerous villages and, after Norwich, it is the most populated area of Norfolk. The north coast belt is an area of wide reclaimed marshland edged by a mixture of salt marsh, sand dunes and shingle banks.

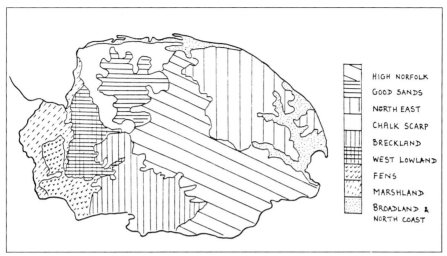

Map C: Areas of Norfolk

The North East, shielded by the Cromer Ridge and the Glaven Valley, is an undulating countryside noted for its rich and fertile glacial loams.

The Good Sands, so-called because of improvements made to the soils of the region during the eighteenth century, was once an area of heath and sheep walks.

The Western Escarpment, sometimes called the Greensand belt, runs from Hunstanton in the north down to the Fens and is bordered on the east by a chalk ridge.

The Marshland is an area stretching from the Wash to the Fens, an area of reclaimed marshland and river silt. It is distinct from the Fens which, like the Broads, is a peat area. The post glacial flood of water covered coastal areas with silts and flooded the marshes to create the Fen country. Drainage in the river valleys was impeded when silts washed down by the floods formed spits across the estuaries. This trapped water helped to turn the layers of dead plants formed over the centuries into peat. This, as will be seen later, was important in the formation of the Broads area.

Breckland covers some 250 square miles bounded by Narborough in the north, Feltwell in the west and Garboldisham in the east. Ranging from 50 to 150 feet above sea level it is an area of sandy soils covering chalk and boulder clay. It is the least densely populated and was once natural heathland.

13

The basic principle of geology is that the earth is continually changing and it is fascinating to conjecture what shape Norfolk will be in the distant future. Will there be another ice age to transform the landscape? Will global warming and the resulting rise in sea levels cause much of Norfolk to be covered by sea once again? Certainly the East Coast Floods of 1953 are an example of what results from a combination of high tides and bad weather. In addition, natural erosion plays a part and there is an example of this on the East coast when the village of Shipden north of Cromer was swallowed up by the sea. Also the formation of spits on the North coast spelt the end of prosperity of ports such as Blakeney and Stiffkey. Here tidal drift moves shingle in two directions. Roughly from Weybourne the drift is westwards but from the Sheringham area the move is south and east.

But man had changed the landscape too and this is the subject of the next chapter.

MAN AND THE LANDSCAPE

OLIVER RACKHAM, in his book 'The History of the Countryside', shows how humans imposed their own influence on the natural environment and in doing so created clearly defined regions. He divided Lowland England into two contrasting regions which he calls Ancient Countryside and Planned Countryside. Norfolk can be divided in this way as is shown by the map on page 19.

Ancient Countryside covers largely mid-Norfolk and the South-East. Here the countryside consists of hamlets and small towns and farms are ancient and remote. Hedges are mixed containing such species as maple and dogwood and they are not straight. Similarly the roads, often sunken, wind, and there are many of them. There are many small woods and pollard trees can be found away from habitation. Antiquities in the area date from different periods and there are usually a maze of footpaths.

The North Coast and West Norfolk form what may be called Planned Countryside. Here large villages are the norm and many farms date from the eighteenth and nineteenth centuries and are built of brick. Hedges are often of hawthorn and are straight, as are the roads which are on the surface, rather than sunken. In this area the walker cannot help noticing that there are fewer footpaths. Antiquities are mainly from the prehistoric period and woods are few and large.

Rackham concludes that Ancient Countryside is 'the product of at least a thousand years of continuity and most of it has altered little since 1700. The other is, in the main, a mass-produced, drawing-board landscape, hurriedly laid out parish by parish under the Enclosure Acts of the eighteenth and nineteenth centuries.' It seems that fortunes were made in true entrepreneurial style in the mass production of plants for 200,000 miles of hedging, the planting of which brought to an end the remaining open-field system in the area. (It is ironic that pressure to produce ever greater tonnage of cereals and other foodstuffs in the 1960s resulted in wholesale destruction of hedges - an event now regretted by many.

The walker may well notice exceptions to the differences listed and even the motorist mentioned in the introduction to this book cannot fail to see how different the landscape is along the A148 compared for instance with that encountered along the A140.
The insights gained on the walk from Saxlingham to Shotesham (Walk 3), for instance, will be very different if compared with those of that from

North Creake (Walk 18). Over the centuries, then, man has converted his Norfolk inheritance into two very contrasting areas.

There are further contrasts which derive from the activities of man in three of the areas listed in the last chapter, namely The Fens, Breckland, and Broadland. These widely differing regions help to make Norfolk such a fascinating county.

Whilst a large part of The Fens lies in the neighbouring counties of Cambridgeshire and Lincolnshire the land between Downham Market and Wisbech, north to Kings Lynn and south to Hockwold, is typical of the area. The Fens are made up of an inland wetland distinct from the coastal marsh hence the division of the area into two - true peaty fenland developing from repeated flooding of surrounding rivers in the south and the non-peaty silt marshland to the north. On the seaward side of the marshland is a third part - the salt marsh cut into twisting creeks and gullies.

The end of the glacial period saw the sea at a lower level than the present wetland but mankind has experienced repeated flooding in the area since it was inhabited. From Neolithic times sea levels have continually fluctuated causing, for instance, extensive flooding in Roman times which spelt the end of an Imperial estate noted for sheep rearing and salt production. The Marshland was flooded twelve times in one century of the Middle Ages and there have been many instances of serious flooding since. At present the coast is sinking in relation to the sea so necessitating a continual review of coastal and river defences.

Several of Norfolk's rivers such as the Nar, the Wissey and the Thet drain from the uplands into the Fens as do several rivers to the west of the county adding to the problem.

There has, therefore, always been a need for drainage and it is Cornelius Vermuyden, supervising the construction of the Old and New Bedford Rivers in 1637 and 1651 and the diversion of the Great Ouse, who immediately springs to mind as being the first to solve the problem. The Old Bedford River stretching from Earith to Denver is 70 feet wide and 21 miles long and the second River was dug parallel to it. Sam's Cut drained the Methwold and Feltwell Fens to the south. This, however, was not the first drainage. The Anglo Saxons before him carried out extensive work which included a 50-mile sea bank extending round the Wash as far as Kings Lynn. Domesday records show that there were a line of settlements extending southwards on the eastern edge of Marshland. By then the population was only two or three people per square mile but three hundred years later this had increased twenty-fold.

Whilst Vermuyden's work still survives as the backbone of the modern drainage system it bequeathed several problems including, initially, a damaged local economy, and a reduction of wildlife. Accumulations of tidal silt were not foreseen and, in addition, drainage gradually caused the shrinkage of the underlying peat and the consequent lowering of the land to the extent that some water courses are now as much as 14 feet above the surrounding land. This resulted in the need to pump floodwater from surrounding drains, first by windmill, then steam and now by electricity, to raise it to the level of the various cuts and rivers.

Floods in 1947 resulted in further major work which included the Cut Off Channel, (originally proposed by Vermuyden in1642!) and the Relief Channel south of Lynn. Banks have also been constructed at a distance from each side of the Levels allowing the land between to be set aside for flooding whenever necessary and these areas are called the Washes. They are now famous for being a centre for migrating birds as well as being a relic of a medieval silt fen, flooded in winter and grazed in the summer. The Fens remains an area at risk; it is significant that large areas are only three feet above the present sea level.

Other visible characteristic features of the area apart from the flatness is the sense of space, straight roads raised above the level of the surrounding countryside, numerous pumping stations, many of which show the three stages of development from wind to electricity, and, in the peat areas, farms and cottages sited on firm ground near rivers. White bricks as well as red are the main building material and pantiles and dutch gables show the Flemish influence.

The second area changed by man's activities is Breckland. Like the rest of the country Breckland was once covered by wildwood, the natural forest that grew following the end of the glacial era. This was the site of the first settlements in Norfolk probably chosen because of the light sandy soil and the nearby availabilty of flints from Grimes Graves. The word breck possibly derives from the Scandinavian 'braec' meaning land cleared for settlement. By the end of the Neolithic period around 2000 B.C. the wildwood of Breckland had vanished. Considering that most native trees are difficult to kill and that felled trees had to be cut up this was no mean 'achievement' when the only tool available was the flint axe. It seems that cleared ground was soon left to grow wild and the area became heathland. That the area was woodless is borne out by Domesday records which show an absence of any 'woody' place names.

The economy of the area then became based on sheep farming and and an industry in the south of rabbit farming. Grazing helped to retain the natural heath by preventing the growth of birch and oak scrub. In the twelfth century the Bishop of Ely set up a huge warren near Lakenheath and other warrens were developed near Thetford. The commercial production of rabbits continued through until 1945. The imposing Thetford Warren Lodge, one of the few remaining buildings used for storing skins and the salted rabbits, showed the original strength of the industry.

The combination of sheep and rabbits gradually led to the erosion of the sandy soil. Evelyn, in his diary, described giant dunes 'rolling from place to place like the sands in the desert of Libya.' Sand storms were frequent leading to the apocryphal story of the Breckland farmer who, when asked whether his farm was in Norfolk or Suffolk, said, 'It depends which way the wind is blowing.' Throughout the area are groves of Scots pine planted to act as wind breaks. They were even used in hedges, their shapes now twisted and stunted by the prevailing wind. The harsh conditions led to depopulation - it is said that there are thirty lost villages - and it is now the least populated part of East Anglia.

By the end of the eighteenth century half of Breckland was still heath and commons but two developments in this century altered this situation. The first was in 1922 when land was acquired by the Forestry Commission near Swaffham and extensive planting of conifer forests began which eventually covered over 80 square miles of Breckland. Depression of agriculture and local poverty meant that owners of the mostly fallow land were eager to sell. It spelt the end of much grazing and rabbit farming, the conversion of much of the remaining natural heathland to forest and the consequent loss of much plant and animal life.

The second development was the Government acquisition of large areas in the south to establish a military training ground. This meant the end for some small hamlets and villages and the restriction of access generally. One benefit, however, has been that this has protected some of the few remaining areas of natural heathland and the wildlife they support.

An aspect of the region which deserves mention is the number of meres. Meres are a feature of Norfolk from North Creake to Diss in the south and groups of them are scattered across Breckland particularly on East Wretham Heath. Some are on private land or in the restricted battle area but one which may be seen is the Devil's Punchbowl, 2½ miles north of Thetford. They are circular in shape and because they are linked to the chalk ground water table the Breckland meres fluctuate, their water level rising or falling.

Another feature of the district are large numbers of pingos but for this see Walk 13.

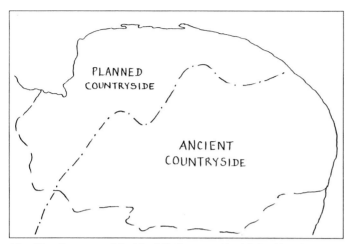

Map D: Character of the Norfolk Countryside. (O.Rackham)

The Broads in the peatlands of east Norfolk were, until forty-five years ago, thought to be natural lakes formed, perhaps, when rivers became silted up. Natural formations elsewhere in Norfolk such as fens and meres have Viking or Saxon names whereas the Broads are named after the neighbouring parishes or local features. Therefore they did not exist in the Saxon era. Research has shown that they are holes left by peat digging carried out in the early Middle Ages. Because parts of Norfolk had been denuded of much of the original wildwood with the consequent shortage of firewood, peat became an alternative fuel. Examination of local records by historians have shown that digging, which may well have started before Domesday, produced something like 12 million turves a year. The kitchens of Norwich Cathedral alone used 400,000 a year! (Rackham)

Investigations found that the Broads are in effect pits with vertical sides that showed different layers down to the strata formed from the original post-glacial wildwood. Up to as much as 10 feet deep, they were divided by walls of peat similar to that of the sides showing that they were man-made pits. The size of many of the Broads indicates the huge operation involved in digging the peat and the manpower that must have been employed. Whilst excavation of the Broads was in progress the sea was at a lower level than it is now and tides would not have caused flooding. The walls that were retained around the pits would have held back excessive river flows. It is thought that a rise in sea levels flooded the workings towards the end of the thirteenth century and this spelt the approaching end of the industry.

The Broads today are a silted up and therefore shrunken version of the originals. Silting is now proceeding at a faster rate than ever and there is also the added problem of phosphates leeching from the surrounding farmland. This together with sewage and the effects of the ever-increasing number of motor boats and launches have destroyed much of the wild plant life and habitat. (Gone are the graceful and slow-moving wherries with their 40 ft tall gaff top sail that were designed to navigate the shallow Broads.) Only one or two private broads remain as they were 50 years ago. Fortunately, a Broads Authority, set up by an Act of 1988 which gave the area National Park status, now co-ordinates restoration and conservation.

Modern drainage plant by River Bure.

A SHORT HISTORY OF THE COUNTY

THE CASUAL OBSERVER looking at a map of England cannot fail to notice how East Anglia projects eastwards into the North Sea rather similar to the carbuncle-like growth to be seen on the trunk of some elderly oak trees. This projection gives to Norfolk a somewhat cut-off appearance from the rest of England and it is probably partly due to this that Norfolk today is less developed than many other areas of England. Whether this will stay true for much longer with the ever-increasing ties with Europe remains to be seen.

For very early man, however, the situation was different - the 'carbuncle' did not exist since England was joined to the continent. Because of the low sea level a land bridge extended eastwards joining East Anglia to the Low Countries. The coast line was further north, and the River Thames joined the River Rhine to flow into the North Sea. Whilst this 'bridge' existed it was possible that Mesolithic man found it just as convenient to hunt in East Anglia as they did further south. There is evidence in the form of hand axes discovered beside earlier river channels, and present river valleys such as the Nar, the Yare and the Thet, that man hunted in Norfolk between the Anglian and Devensian ice ages. They probably chose the beginning and ends of interglacial periods when the climate would have been more temperate. The Hoxnian interglacial which lasted 40,000 years is so called because, from brick pits at Hoxne in the north of Suffolk only a mile from the boundary with Norfolk, was evidence in the form of charcoal sediments which indicated that fires had been lit possibly to ward off wildlife. In addition, pollen remains proved the existence of a mixed forest and a varied plant life only possible in a warmer climate.

Around 8300 B.C. when the glaciers were beginning to retreat and Norfolk was still the western extremity of the European coastline there is evidence of some farming communities on the North coast. A rich site was discovered at Titchwell and at Kelling. Had these people struggled across land or had they come by sea? Did they choose these sites because attack could only really come from the sea? Then the sea level would have been sixty metres below the land and the sites would have been in a commanding position.

By about 6500 B.C. Norfolk's coastline was much as it is today and there was little difference in the physical landscape except for river courses and estuaries. The warmer climate had led to the melting of the glaciers, the resulting rise in sea levels had submerged the land bridge and England had become an island.

The warm period encouraged the growth of thick forest or 'wildwood' especially on the heavier soils which presented a problem for Neolithic or New Stone Age Man as they discovered the advantage of herding animals and cultivating land rather than hunting. To achieve this the forest had to be cut down and the only tool available was the flint axe. Research has shown that it was possible to cut down a softwood tree 15 cm in diameter in about five minutes with a flint axe. The source of much of the flint was Grimes Graves (see page34).
Some forest clearance took place at this time particularly on the lighter soils such as the Breckland area and in the north. Indeed, axes found throughout Norfolk show the presence of farmers during this period. Many flint axes have been discovered at Spong Hill near N.Elmham and large numbers of arrow heads too in Breckland which may indicate that farmers had to protect their settlements from intruders. Certainly, Breckland was cleared of natural forest and cultivated at an early date, starting about 4000 B.C.. Some heathlands had developed during the Iron Age.

That the area saw a lot of activity between the Neolithic period and the Iron Age can be judged not only by the existence of the Icknield Way but also by long barrows and later by many Bronze Age round barrows - well over 600. Very few of these are found on the heavy land of central Norfolk except in the valleys of the River Yare and Wensum. (Only 200 or so have survived the hand of the plough).

The sharper tools that Iron Age man possessed not only increased the clearance of remaining forest but also enabled the production of stronger ploughshares that were capable of working the heavier soils of central Norfolk. The quantities of coins found in N.W.Norfolk together with the existence of forts at Holkham, Warham (see Walk 6), and S.Creake (where there was a fort three times larger than Warham which was destroyed by ploughing) show that the area was a centre for the Iceni tribe, one of whose leaders, Boadicca, was to cause the Roman authorities so much concern. By the first century A.D. large parts of Norfolk were settled. It is possible that Thetford was the 'capital' and that the present southern boundary of Norfolk the Little Ouse and the River Waveney, was set.

By the time of the Roman Occupation there was an established network of settlements and tracks which the Romans made use of and developed. It is thought that Peddars Way originated between 70 and 100 A.D. and may have been planned to link with a ferry crossing the Wash. Other roads from Colchester to Caistor St Edmund (Venta Icenorium) their administrative capital and from the Fens to the east coast passing near Reepham (Walk 8) were constructed. Another, which can be traced on the map, is that from Holkham to Toftrees. To guard against renewed trouble with the Iceni the

Romans built a signal station at Thornham - to link with the ninth Legion at Lincoln - and forts in the centre of the county at Ashill and Threxton.

The majority of Romans lived in the countryside in villas and farmsteads. Sixteen villas have been identified, many strung along the Icknield Way. A fall in the sea levels at this time led to the Fenland becoming drier and the area became an Imperial estate rearing sheep and producing salt. Sites of villas have also been discovered at Gayton Thorpe and Grimston east of Kings Lynn, the centres for working farms. They contrasted with the 'posh' villas that were sited in the Methwold and Feltwell areas. In the third century with Burgh Castle now, four miles inland, a fort was built at Caister on Sea and at Brancaster and Cromer. Presumably the threat of Saxon invasion from the continent was a very real one even then.

The Saxons possibly chose the Wash or Breydon Water as the easiest landfalls for the early invasions.

The Roman roads remained important links for the incoming Saxons as evidenced by the defensive banks and ditches constructed during the fifth century, all of which crossed Roman roads. One, Launditch, later became the name of one of the Saxon Hundreds. The heritage bequeathed to us from the Saxons lies perhaps most importantly in the Christianisation of East Anglia and in the social and political organisation of the country. They took over an already developed countryside of farms and fields, villages and roads but superimposed their culture. By the seventh century a complex society was established with a king, and different classes of people from nobles down to freemen and slaves. Early Saxon settlements were adjacent to rivers as at Shropham, Bridgham and Wretham; 'ham' meant a village or estate usually sited on well drained soil. Most large villages merited the suffix 'ham'; and some were later to become market towns like Aylsham and Wymondham. The uplands too were settled. A large settlement existed at Spong Hill near Elmham where a cemetery in use during the fifth and sixth centuries contained over 2000 cremation pots.

By 680 Christianity was well established in Norfolk. King Raedwald had been converted by St Augustine and his son Sigbert encouraged St Felix in his missionary work. A granddaughter of Sigbert established a monastery at Dereham. East Anglia was divided and the northern 'See' was initially at North Elmham and later, after the conversion of the Danes, at Thetford. Obviously, because the majority of Saxon churches would have been built of wood, many did not survive but there are still about forty churches with identifiable Saxon features in Norfolk today. A Norman church lies on the site of many a wooden Saxon one.

Pottery remains show that by the ninth century two thirds of the parishes in Norfolk were in existence, and most of modern place names, although the sites of villages may have since moved.

Later settlement was densest on the heavier rich soils of south, east and mid-Norfolk. It was in these areas that the estates of freemen were established especially in the district of Flegg which was settled by the Danes. There, place names ending in 'by', of which there are over twenty, signified a village; 'thorpe' like the Saxon 'tun' (ton) usually meant an outlying farmstead which later developed into a village itself. The Danish influence is also found, for example, in the suffix 'gate' meaning street as in Pottergate in Norwich and in a name to the south of Norwich which perhaps shows the wit of the Saxons, Newton Flotman, 'flottmann' being the Saxon name for a Dane. Some villages shared a name later differentiated by the name of the church or by its geographical position, north, south or east. Other names developed from topographical features such as Burnham or its connection with agriculture. 'Leah' (ley) signified a clearing in the woods which, incidently, indicated what once was an area of forest. The names of Somerton and Winterton have obvious origins.

The origin of towns is an interesting one. Reed, in his book, suggests that a town may be so called when it becomes a focus for trade and when it can support a variety of skills and trades needed by the surrounding populace.

Map E: The Norfolk Hundreds

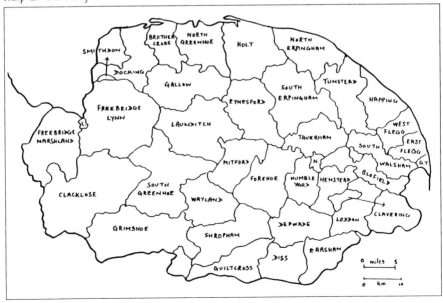

24

In the ninth century there were important settlements both at Thetford and Northwic (Norwich). Thetford is mentioned in documents of 870 and Northwic appears for the first time on coins of Aethelstan 920-40. Thetford had its own mint by 960 and was a centre for bronze and iron ware and pottery. Like Norwich it was to experience repeated sacking by the Danes.

After the Norman invasion about sixty men, eight of whom were bishops and abbots, held land on behalf of the King who had estates in 170 parishes. In Norwich the Normans established their own enclave in what is now the St Peter Mancroft area and they destroyed 100 houses to make room for the castle. Herbert de Losinga, the bishop of Elmham moved the See from Thetford to Norwich and founded the Cathedral in 1096. 'Within fifty years of the Conquest the Normans did more to alter the layout of Norwich than their successors did in the next five hundred years.' (S.Wade Martins)

The boundary of modern Norfolk is almost identical to that of 1086 except for some variations on the southern boundary. 731 place names are mentioned in Domesday, the majority of which still exist today. A few have disappeared or are unidentifiable, some coastal villages like Shipden near Cromer have been eroded by the sea and some have been merged with another.

One facet of Norfolk soon noticed by a visitor is the number of villages with similar names. There are seven Burnhams for example, three Barshams, three Wrethams, three Birchams and numerous pairs of villages like the Snorings and the Buckenhams. Exactly when these achieved separate identities is varied and sometimes obscure but the reason for their existence usually lies in the fact that the large estates, handed over as rewards after the Norman invasion, were later divided up and each part took their name from the original centre of the estate. Some, like the Buckenhams, (Walk 1) owed their separate identity to the whim of the landowner, in this case a Norman lord who wished to build a new castle and founded New Buckenham.

By the time of the Domesday survey in 1086 Norfolk was one of the most populated areas of England and certainly the richest.
The survey recorded a high number of freemen and three and a half plough teams to the square mile, both indications of the wealth of the area. Over 46,000 sheep were recorded outnumbering pigs by more than twenty to one. There were far fewer cattle. Of the 731 settlements 302 had a water mill, some having more than one. The administrative system of 'hundreds' evolved by the Anglo-Saxons was continued and they survived, although with diminished powers in the nineteenth century, until 1974 (see map on

page 24). It looks as though the larger hundreds were originally the poorer and less populated areas.

The majority of parishes that exist today were recorded then and it is possible that the ecclesiastical parish was also identical to the secular ownership of the land and therefore the unit of government. For some reason not all the churches are mentioned - only 217 are listed - those dedicated to Saxon saints for example were ignored. The multiplicity of churches in some parishes is evident even in 1086. Of 37 parishes with two churches 22 were mentioned in the survey. By the thirteenth century there are 790 churches and many parishes had more than one. There were three at Warham, four at Shotesham, and nine at the Burnhams, seven of them within 1½ miles. At Reepham there were three in the same churchyard. Again the division of large estates is often the reason with the new landowners competing with each other by having their own church. The churches are therefore good guides to the sites of early settlements bearing in mind that many that we see today replaced earlier buildings.

The medieval period was a flourishing time for church building. Despite periods of economic decline over 900 were built and two-thirds of these are still used today. Over 60 churches have Norman doorways of which the one at Hales is a beautiful example (Walk 2). Even the hard life of the Fens in the later Middle Ages did not deter the building of magnificent churches such as those at Terrington and Walpole. Sir John Betjeman sums up our heritage. 'Norfolk would not be Norfolk without a church tower on the horizon or round a corner up a lane. We cannot spare a single church. When a church has been pulled down the country seems empty or is like a necklace with a jewel missing.'

One feature of interest is the many churches with round towers - over 100. The majority of these are in the south-east because that was where the majority of the population were in the early Middle Ages. Why round towers were built has provoked some argument. Some say that it was the lack of local stone to form the quoins but others argue that it was harder to build a round tower. A.Heywood in 'An Historical Atlas of Norfolk' suggests that they were built for cultural reasons; areas of north Germany, from where Anglo Saxons originated, also have buildings with round towers.

Throughout Norfolk there are a number of churches which can be seen standing alone perhaps in the middle of a field, or on a hill with little evidence of past dwellings in the vicinity other than perhaps a farm. Many have assumed that the community they served died out as a result of the Black Death but in many cases there are more likely reasons. Poor soil making subsistence impossible, encroachment by the sea, the creation of parks in the eighteenth century or a more thriving, nearby parish are some (see Walk 20).

Monasteries and friaries were also an integral part of medieval life. There were over a hundred religious houses during the Middle Ages including the first Benedictine abbey of St Benet outside Norwich. Some buildings still survive at Castle Acre, Binham and Thetford and Greyfriars at Little Walsingham still stands as a reminder that the village was the largest centre of pilgrimage in the twelfth and thirteenth centuries. Henry III visited here on a tour which took in Dereham, Castle Acre and a shrine at Broomholm on the East Coast before returning to St Benet's Abbey and Norwich, a tour which lasted eleven days, which itself was a testimony to the road system of the time.

A large proportion of land in the Middle Ages was common land, either heath, woodland or green. By the end of the eighteenth century only one sixth, 20,000 acres, remained. Today only a fraction of this exists. Mousehold Heath, the scene of rebellion during the Peasant's Revolt, once extended almost as far as Hoveton; now only a fragment remains surrounded by housing. Kelling Heath and the commons at New Buckenham and Mulbarton are examples of happier survivals.

Castles are not such a feature of Norfolk as in other counties. Apart from Norwich the only notable remains are at Thetford, Castle Acre and the keep at Castle Rising. Was it the lack of local stone or was Norfolk man more peaceable after Hereward's time? Most Norman defensive sites were in the form of motte and bailey castles which were quick to build and easily removed. Later in the Middle Ages defended houses were built instead and owners of property sported moats but less as a defensive measure than as a status symbol or perhaps to stock fish.

Small towns such as Swaffham and Aylsham probably achieved importance from the grant of market charters. Only three markets, of which Holt was one, are mentioned in Domesday but by 1300 there were over 120 mainly in High Norfolk and the east. There was a gradual decline and by 1700 only a quarter remained. The ports of Lynn and Yarmouth prospered from the trade in corn and wool respectively.

Economic changes led to periodic decline and unrest. The Peasants' Revolt saw a group from Bury threatening to burn Thetford and there was unrest in Breckland but the main disturbance centred in the north-east when an 'army' gathered on Mousehold Heath near Norwich. It was led by Geoffrey Litster who, on the collapse of the rebellion, was executed. They

27

were protesting amongst other things against tax collection and the presence of Flemish settlers. During the fifteenth century enclosures of open fields were common in some areas and large sheep farms were being developed. At East Barsham, for instance, Sir Henry Fermor owned over 15,000 sheep divided into 20 flocks. A better organised rebellion caused by these developments occurred in 1549. An army of 10,000 gathered again on Mousehold Heath and there was another camp at Downham Market. Norwich was briefly captured in August but the army was routed three days later by an army led by the Earl of Warwick aided by mercenary cavalry from Germany. (An excellent account of this event can be found in Tom Pocock's book).

A hundred years later the county was not greatly affected by the Civil War with under a third of the gentry involved. Parliamentarians outnumbered the Royalists roughly by two to one although active families were often equally divided. The Pastons and the Heydons, for example, were for the King and the Hobarts from Blickling, the Astleys and the Cokes were for Parliament. Royalists were strong in the south and in Kings Lynn. Tenant farmers probably followed their landlord. Labourers and cottagers, a great proportion of whom were poor, suffered as they always do in times of war and unless they were pressed into service as a foot soldier, probably had little allegiance either way. Bearing in mind the Norfolkman's independent nature it is a wonder that Cromwell's Model Army, many of whom were recruited from East Anglia, was so efficient.

There was one event which would have made the headlines in modern newspapers. In 1648 in Norwich occurred 'The Great Blowe'. A house belonging to the Parliamentarians was being looted during a period of unrest in the town caused by Puritan restrictions. A magazine stored in the house blew up causing deaths and occasioning a riot.

For two hundred years after the Restoration there was stability and the agricultural revolution that centred in Norfolk with the reforms of Lord 'Turnip' Townshend and Thomas Coke of Holkham, later Earl of Leicester, helped to bring improvements especially into the north-east and the Good Sands regions. There was, however, a down side with occasional unrest caused again by enclosures which were not always to the benefit of the farm labourer and there was a lot of unemployment. Even Lord Nelson was moved to write and complain about the lot of the landless labourer 'in want of everything to make their life comfortable'.

The period was one of great rebuilding and saw the construction of some of the country's great houses particularly in the north and west where the land was less fertile and less expensive. The fertile soils of High Norfolk and its long farming history had resulted in the building of many halls and large houses dating from the late middle ages to the seventeenth century, many of them timber framed. Elsewhere brick and pebble were the main materials and pantiles, brought from Holland as ballast, were a common roofing material. The Stuart reign had already produced some large mansions, notably Blickling commenced in 1619. It was designed by Robert Lyminge of Hatfield fame for Sir Henry Hobart, the Lord Chief Justice. Raynham was built about the same time and brick and lime kilns were constructed on the estate for the purpose. Then in 1722 Houghton was commenced for Sir Robert Walpole, the first Prime Minister of England, and this was followed by Holkham. By the middle of the nineteenth century estates of 1000 acres or more covered half of Norfolk, only a few of these being in the east of the county.

Geometrical layouts for gardens were first the norm but in the late eighteenth century naturalism was the vogue and the next hundred years saw the development of many large parks. Two million trees were planted at Holkham in the last twenty years of the century and lakes were constructed here and at Blickling. Much later, in 1860, a house in Sandringham was bought by Prince Edward who had it much enlarged. Industrial magnates of the early part of this century completed the process with houses such as Kelling and Beachamwell.

Perhaps one of the most important developments to change the face of Norfolk in modern times was that of the railways. The county had a good network of roads, albeit poor in winter, although not many had become turnpikes. Celia Fiennes recorded that Norfolk miles were long and the roads were 'pretty deep especially after raine'. A wagon loaded with sacks of grain would take two days to travel from Norwich to Lynn. Despite improvements to canals the large number of wherries plying the water-ways were slow-moving although they were capable of carrying large loads. The advent of railways, however, with the first line from Norwich to Yarmouth completed in 1844 and the first London link three years later, put the county on the map as far as trade and later tourism was concerned. Other lines followed which were instrumental in the development of resorts such as Cromer and Hunstanton. Railways were still being constructed in the last years of the nineteenth century. The Midland and Great Northern Joint Railway, later known as The Muddle and Get Nowhere Line, was set up in 1893, the main yards being at Melton Constable where terraces were built for the railway workers.

No longer were villagers dependent upon the nearest market town for all their needs and the towns, previously dependent upon supplying the needs of agriculture, began to attract other industries. By the late 1950s most places were within five miles of a railway station but this was to change dramatically with the Beeching recommendations a decade later. Now only a few main lines survive.

Another more modern development which helped to change the face of the countryside was the construction during World War II of nearly fifty airfields in East Anglia, the majority of which were in Norfolk. Many have since become redundant and have either reverted to farmland or have become bases for light industry.

HISTORICAL EVENTS IN NORFOLK

c400,000 B.C.	Presence of hunters during temperate era - flints found in river valleys.
c8300 B.C.	Farming communities on the north coast between glaciations.
c6500 B.C.	The land bridge to the continent is submerged and Britain becomes an island.
4000 B.C.	Breckland is cleared of the natural 'wildwood'.
2000 B.C.	The industry at Grimes Graves in progress. There are settlements at Weeting and Brandon. Long barrows at Broome Heath, Harpley. Over 620 Round barrows in the county, 220 still visible.
500 B.C.	A late Iron Age fort exists at Gallows Hill, Warham and at South Creake. A farmstead at West Harling.
100 B.C.	The Iceni tribal centre is in the North West Norfolk area. Forts at Holkham, Warham and South Creake.
A.D. 70	Early Roman forts at Threxton, Ashill, Horstead. The planned town of Caistor St Edmund and Peddars Way are established.
200	Caistor is fortified. Forts also built at Brancaster, Crome and Burgh (in Suffolk prior to boundary changes). There is a large settlement at Brettenham and farm estates astride the Icknield Way and Peddars Way.
410	Roman rule ends.
680	A Large Saxon settlement at Spong Hill and nearby cemetery contains over 2000 cremation pots. Christianity established in East Anglia. Bishopric at North Elmham.
870	Vikings occupy Thetford.
880	Norwich market begins.
870 - 920	Norfolk under Danish control.
917	Edward the Elder defeats the Danes.
920 - 40	Northwic (Norwich) appears on coins in Athelstan's reign.
960	Thetford has own mint. Sacked in 993 as was Norwich.
1004 - 10	Thetford is burnt.
c1080	The Normans establish their own zone in Norwich in the St Peter Mancroft area. 100 houses are destroyed to make room for the first castle.
1086	Norfolk's population is c125,000. No woodland existed in half the settlements listed in Domesday. 33 Norfolk Hundreds mentioned.

1095	An East Anglian diocese of Norfolk and Suffolk is founded.
1096	Norwich Cathedral commenced.
1226	The King visits Walsingham, the largest centre for pilgrimage in the twelfth and thirteenth centuries.
1287	Floods herald the end of peat digging and the formation of the Broads.
1334	Norwich is the sixth richest town in England.
1347	Grey Friars established at Walsingham.
1349	The Black Death hits Norwich and again in the 1360s.
1370	The first of the Lollards, a priest from Lynn, is burnt at the stake.
1381	The Peasants' Revolt reaches Norfolk. Thetford is threatened. A crowd gathers on Mousehole Heath. Revolt is quashed by Bishop Despencer in a battle near North Walsham.
1522	Norwich pays £749 in tax to help finance Henry VIII's war with France.
1531	Thomas Bilney burnt in Norwich.
1549	Kett's rebellion. 10,000 camp outside Norwich and later capture the town. The army was finally routed in a battle at Dussindale, Thorpe St Andrew.
1600	The population of Norwich reaches 15,000.
1603	Archbishop Whitgift orders count of the number of communicants in the Church.
1609	Disastrous floods on the East Coast.
1619	The building of Blickling commences for Sir Henry Hobart.
1622	'Turnip' Townshend commences the building of Raynham Hall.
1630	Construction of the Old Bedford River to drain the Fens.
1634	Edward Coke, Attorney General, spends £10,000 to purchase monastic lands and lay the foundation of the great Holkham estate.
1643	Norwich raises £60,000 in taxes for the Parliament cause. Lynn is besieged throughout August.
1646	King Charles I arrives at Downham Market and moves to Mundford. There is a riot in Norwich.
1651	The New Bedford River is dug.
1661	Miles Corbett, a Yarmouth M.P. and one of the signatories of the King's death warrant, is hanged at Tyburn as a regicide. Yarmouth celebrates the first Lent since the war.
1695	One of the first Turnpike Acts passed is for the Wymondham to Attleborough section of the present A11.
1722	The building of Houghton Hall started for Sir Robert Walpole.

1745	John Wesley pays his first visit to Norwich. By 1790 he has made 40 visits to the county.
1764	Holkham completed by Thomas Coke.
1776	Annual sheep shearing held at Holkham. The Southdown breed introduced.
1779	Ransomes founded.
1800	Three quarters of the county's medieval woodland are lost during the last 200 years.
1801	Norfolk's population 273,000.
1808	Ransomes introduce the first universal plough.
1816	Riots at Watton, Downham Market and Norwich. Two executed.
1826	North Walsham and Dilham Canal cut.
1835-7	More than 3,000 from Norfolk emigrate to Canada.
1844	Norfolk's first railway from Norwich to Yarmouth.
1848	Burrell's make the first successful threshing machine.
1850	Cholera epidemic in Norwich. Cromer becomes a fashionable resort. Railway from Norwich extended to Cromer in 1877.
1851	Norfolk's population 443,000.
1854	Colmans Mustard factory opens in Norwich. Over 200 boot and shoe firms in Norwich.
1870	Sandringham purchased by Prince Edward, later Edward VII.
1889	The County Council assumes responsibility for the roads.
1891	Norfolk's population 468,800.
1906	Eastern Counties Agricultural Labour Union founded.
1911	Herring Industry at its height in Yarmouth.
1912	First sugar beet grown in Norfolk. Factory at Cantley opened in 1921.
1923	First Council estate in Norwich.
1920	Norwich ring road started.
1944	Over 100 airfields operational in Norfolk.
1950	New relief channel constructed at Denver.
1951	Norfolk's population 548,000
1968	The North coast is created an Area of Outstanding Natural Beauty.
1971	Norfolk's population 626,800.
1974	Norfolk's coastline created a Heritage Coast.
1990	The Broads obtain National Park status.
1991	Norfolk's population 745,613. Norwich - 120,000.

TRADE AND INDUSTRY IN NORFOLK

NORFOLK'S PROSPERITY relied in the past, as it does today, upon agriculture from the time when the first clearances of wildwood took place through the centuries to the present scene of large, highly mechanised farms.   It is possible to claim, however, that the earliest industry in the county was that of flint mining because flint tools used in the Neolithic era enabled man to clear the forest and establish settled farming communities. Grimes Graves, now hidden in the forest north of Thetford, was the centre of a mining industry for flints which was at its height about 2000 B.C..

The site was discovered by Canon Greenwell who, in 1868, proved that the many hollows in the area were infilled sites of mines. Over 700 shafts were dug over an 80 acre site, each of the shafts between 4 and 8 metres deep. To dig each shaft antler picks were used; from remains found on the site it is estimated that between 100 and 150 picks were used to dig each shaft and to extract the flint embedded in bands in the chalk. Discoveries of flint tools that originated from other areas such as Cornwall and the Lake District show that there must have been considerable trade across the country in this ware and, no doubt, in other commodities. (I have not been able to learn whether flints from Grimes Graves found their way to more distant parts.)

The industry was later reborn to satisfy the demand for flints by the British Army. At the height of the Napoleonic wars in 1804 a monthly supply of a quarter of a million flints were needed and ten years later this figure had quadrupled.

Artifacts discovered in Norfolk made from both copper and bronze and dating from the Bronze Age between 2500 and 800 B.C. are of high quality and indicate that there was a sizeable population in the area with advance techniques in smelting.

Clearance of forest went on apace as arable farming and the development of pasture land increased. Crops of bread wheat, and barley and rye for malting, were grown and pigs were husbanded with goats and some deer. Eggs were another staple food. It is not till the seventeenth century that there is any record of Norfolk turkeys!

Fish was an important part of the diet and early settlements were beside rivers partly for this reason. There were many fisheries in the Fens and the Romans established salt pans to preserve the produce. Herring, cod and eel were fished and, by the time of Domesday, fishing and rabbit farming formed staple industries.

The early beginnings of Great Yarmouth were possibly as a camping ground for fishermen. As a fishing port it was to reach its zenith in the first years of this century when the herring industry was exporting a third of a million barrels of fish a year and employing five thousand workers. North coast towns like Sheringham and Cromer were important ports in the Middle Ages. Later with the introduction of the crab pot in the 1860s the industry in shell fish took off to such an extent that an Act was passed to limit size of catch. (Common Market restrictions in 1996 are not a new phenomenon!)

By Domesday there were over 46,000 sheep to be recorded and flocks continued to be an important part of the economy although enclosures prior to introducing flocks were a cause of discontent. One of Thomas Coke's improvements at the end of the eighteenth century was the intro-duction of the Southdown breed. Later enclosure, such as during the Napoleonic wars, was to increase the amount of arable land. In the twentieth century sheep farming was to decline dramatically during the inter-war years when there was a corresponding rise in arable farming (encouraged by subsidies for wheat), in dairy farming and, in areas like the Fens and Flegg, the development of orchards and market gardens.

By the end of the nineteenth century Norfolk had 44 iron founders whose work was largely associated with agricultural machinery. Further mecha-nisation in the 1950s caused a dramatic decline in the numbers of horses and therefore of associated trades such as saddlers and smiths.

At present four fifths of the land in the county is used for agriculture. Cereals remain, as they were in the time of the first settled communities, the main crop with half of all Norfolk's arable land devoted to it. Pigs also continue their long association with Norfolk - pig breeding in the county is nearly ten per cent of the national population. Sugar beet was first grown experimentally in 1912 and the county now grows just under a third of the national crop. Poultry, vegetables and greenhouse crops are other impor-tant aspects of Norfolk's agricultural production and new crops like flax and lavender have been added.

Many industries which flourished in the past have disappeared or are shadows of their former selves. The manufacture of textiles was perhaps the most important industry after agriculture. Norfolk was the chief centre of the manufacture of worstead material, much of which was exported through Yarmouth. Linen was another local product from hemp grown in the valleys of the Waveney and the Little Ouse.

There were once 114 brickyards making the county the fourth largest producer in the country. Over 100 parishes had their own brickyard and some had more than one. Large herds of cattle in the sixteenth century resulted in a thriving tanning industry especially around Norwich, and this in turn encouraged the rise of the boot and shoe factories of which there were over 200 in the second half of the nineteenth century. Many of these were in Norwich which at that time was also famous, among other things, for the production of shawls and crepe and, of course, mustard.

By 1900 the railways were an important part of the scene linking the three main centres with London, with the largest market towns and with the increasingly important coastal resorts. In doing so they changed the character of the county reducing the need for small communities to be self-supporting and opening the county to the outside world - a boon for food producers and tourists alike, and a process later completed with the mass ownership of the motor car.

In the last quarter of the twentieth century new industries have sprung up: fish curing and food processing firms and their associated packaging, and engineering companies which deal with a range of products ranging from sugar to peas and crab meat; chemical manufacturers, insurance firms, H.M.S.O. and educational suppliers all represent the diversity of the industrial and commercial scene. Whilst a fishing fleet still operates from Yarmouth the port is also important for being a major supply base for the North Sea gas industry for which there is a terminal at Bacton. At the time of writing an undersea pipeline is planned to supply gas from the terminal to Holland.

Today Lynn and Yarmouth complement the strong link forged with Europe by the port of Felixstowe (Suffolk) and the local economy benefits from the links with Europe as it did when the wool and cloth trade was at its height. Norwich Airport reinforces the link. The land bridge which connected the county to Europe over eight thousand years ago has been forged in yet another way.

THE NATURAL ENVIRONMENT

PREVIOUS CHAPTERS have already described how our geology formed the differing regions of Norfolk and how, in three areas particularly, human beings have been responsible for the considerable changes resulting in the countryside we experience today. This, in turn, has affected the nature and range of wildlife that inhabits the three areas and it is interesting to conjecture what natural life might have existed in those areas had the changes not taken place. What, for instance, might the environment of the Broads offer had the medieval peat industry been uneconomic? Has peat digging resulted in a richer natural environment than would have existed if it had never taken place? The draining of the Fens was obviously essential if repeated flooding was to be avoided, but the development of the Ouse Washes has shown what, with hindsight, could have been achieved over a wider area. The few remaining areas of natural Breckland are examples of what has been lost in past centuries.

Perhaps Norfolk's coastline, continually evolving through accretion and erosion, is the one area of the county where man's influence has been the least. Here, weather and tidal patterns are dominant in forming spits, destroying cliffs, and creating marshes and dunes.

The Weather

It is well known that both Norfolk and Suffolk are the driest areas of the British Isles - an encouraging factor for walkers. England is at its widest from the west coast across to Norfolk and the prevailing westerlies that exist throughout the year have shed most of their moisture by the time they reach the county. Average annual rainfall in the British Isles is approximately 42" whilst in Norfolk it is 23" (Wales and Scotland have 52"). Over the years it appears that the Swaffham and Aylsham areas of the county have the highest rainfall with 27" and the north coastal strip from the Wash to Wells the lowest. East Anglia's rainfall is generally split evenly between the first and second halves of the year with October tending to have the lowest of any month. So, as well as influencing its development, Norfolk's bulge affects its weather.

The cold North Sea also contributes to varying weather patterns along the 90 mile coastline; often when the rest of the country is experiencing warm sunny weather the coastal areas are dull and cool with mist or onshore winds.

The south westerly airstream can, though, result in the North Norfolk coast being the hottest part of the country, but with Norfolk's coastline facing in three directions, conditions at Holme, for instance, can be very different from those at Happisburgh.

Extremes of temperature are more often experienced in the spring and early summer but the range of temperature during winter is not wide. True to the weather rhyme, the highest winds do blow in March although during the winter months they tend to be more moderate compared to the rest of the country. Country people call the East wind 'a lazy wind' - instead of blowing round, it blows straight through! Since they bring with them Siberian temperatures they can be exceedingly cold. Heavy snowfalls tend to occur only in north Norfolk. Spring, the peak period for north-east and east winds, therefore, is often a cold season. July tends to be the month for most thunderstorms.

In summary, the weather in Norfolk is ideal for the walker. Perhaps I have been lucky - I have rarely experienced rain whilst walking in the county. Possibly the need to pack a sweater outweights the need for waterproofs!

Rivers

Apart from the coastline, Norfolk's rivers figure large among its natural features. As can be seen from a map their watershed is the centre of the county with the majority flowing east or north to the coast and a few, the Nar, the Wissey and the Little Ouse flowing west to join the Great Ouse on its way to the Wash. The river Bure with its tributaries, the Ant and Thurne, joins the river Yare, itself supplemented by the Wensum and Tas, to flow into the broad expanse of Breydon Water and thence to the sea. None are any great width and all move leisurely on their way seawards.

Wildlife

A glance at the list of nature reserves on pages 115-117 leads to an appreciation of the wealth of natural habitat and wildlife that is in the county. From the Wash to Weybourne there are a string of reserves which care for the natural environment, protecting the dunes and marshes and providing a haven for a wide variety of wintering, migrant and summer visiting birds. Much of the land to the west and east of Kings Lynn has been reclaimed for agriculture but the marshes and the mud flats of the Wash are a major wintering ground for waders. The R.S.P.B. reserve at Snettisham overlooks tidal mudflats and old gravel workings. From Holme to Weybourne there are only a few gaps between reserves and the whole coast is designated an Area of Outstanding Natural Beauty.

Woods in the Sandringham area, at Holkham and Wells are home for a variety of birds such as crossbill and nuthatch and many summer visitors.

Along the coast sea and wind have created dunes and these in turn have helped in the formation of salt marshes on the landward side with many winding creeks and mudflats - a refuge and feeding ground for birds and a haven for a variety of marsh plants. The shingle ridges are a nesting ground for terns and a foothold for plants such as sea rocket, the yellow-horned poppy, sea holly and sea kale.

The following calendar gives a taste of the variety of birds to be seen along the coast.

Winter to early Spring - divers, grebe, eider, cormorants, hen harriers, snowbuntings and flocks of sheldrake.

May - Godwits, Knot, Spotted Redshank, Golden Plover and vagrants such as hoopoe and bluethroats.

June and July - Sandwich and Little Terns breed, Marsh Harriers and Bearded Tits active, Greenshank and Whimbrel.

September - Long-eared owls and Water Rails. Easterly winds bring in African migrants.

October onwards - Large flocks of duck, geese and swans arrive for the winter to join wintering waders, godwit, knot, dunlin and grey plover. For a detailed description of the wildlife of the area, Peter and Margaret Clarke's book can hardly be bettered.

Slightly further inland in West Norfolk, Ringstead Downs, Syderstone and Roydon Commons provide a varied habitat for plants, animals and insects. Ringstead Downs is one of the few areas of chalk grassland in Norfolk and home to chalk-loving plants and butterflies. The acid heath of Syderstone Common descends to a valley with pools in which natterjack toads and other amphibians can be seen. Several species of butterfly thrive there. Heathland and boggy plants, dragonflies, curlew and nightjar can be seen at Roydon Common.

In Breckland, where reclamation for agriculture and later forestry have changed the nature of the area, Weeting Heath and East Wretham Heath are two rare examples of surviving Breckland heath which were once part of large areas of heavily grazed land. The former supports many plants, some of which can be found in few places in the country such as spiked speedwell and Breckland mugwort. It is also the only site where stone curlew can be seen. East Wretham supports a range of plants and is home to scarce spiders as well as a variety of butterflies such as the small skipper and brown argus. The heath is also known for its meres (see page 116).

Also in Breckland are New Buckenham and Thompson Commons. The latter is an important site on account of the pingos (see Walk 13) and the plants they support. Many species of dragonfly breed on the pingos and the meadows and woodland of the Common are a habitat for wildflowers and butterflies including the White Admiral. New Buckenham Common (Walk 1) is an example of unimproved grassland, never ploughed, and used originally by the villagers for grazing. It hosts a mass of wild flowers including, in early summer, the green winged orchid.

The wide area of Broadland once supported a teeming wildlife but unfortunately the decline of Broadland crafts which used the local resources of wood and reed led to the silting up of dykes. Fens became overgrown with dense alder. Surrounding land was reclaimed for agriculture, crops have replaced grazing and the consequent need for fertilisers has resulted in the draining of chemicals into the dykes and rivers. In turn, the rich nutrients have encouraged the growth of algae which blocks the development of native plants and animals. This, and the ever growing traffic of the tourist craft on the waterways causing erosion, has killed the natural life of many of the broads.

Fortunately, various organisations have established reserves where natural life has been maintained or, in some cases, restored. Now at Cockshoot Broad, for instance, coot, heron and grebe can be seen and white water lilies provide a base for damselflies. Many of the Broad reserves support dragonflies and damselflies and the swallowtail butterfly which lay their eggs on milk parsley. Alderfen and Hickling Broads are good places to observe wildfowl and the latter has a visitor centre and a series of trails leading to different habitats of broad, fen and grazing marsh. Upton Fen is one of the best places to see fenland plants.

Woodland

The clearance of natural forest in Breckland was by no means remedied by the planting of the conifer forests earlier this century. Luckily a later policy of planting broad-leaf trees on the boundaries of conifer plantations has led to an increase of wildlife, and amenity areas such as that near Santon Downham (Suffolk) provide good sites for woodland birds.

Very little old forest survives in Norfolk. Domesday records that out of over twelve thousand settlements only half possessed any woodland. There was no woodland in the Fens. Much later the county lost three-quarters of its surviving medieval woods to agriculture and development during the seventeenth and eighteenth centuries.

Out of several woodland reserves in Norfolk today, Foxley Wood is the largest remaining ancient woodland with a recorded history back to the Norman Conquest. The wood is particularly rich in grasses and flowering plants which are also hosts to a variety of insects and butterflies. Wayland Wood is another example of ancient woodland and has a superb display of flowering plants from Spring onwards. The ancient pollard trees of Thursford Wood are a home for fungi and rare lichens. Honeypot Wood on the chalky boulder clay of mid-Norfolk is a wood which has been coppiced for many years and also has the medley of plants to be found in an ancient woodland.

Hedges

A few references have been made in the walks of Hooper's rule (see Walk 3). The rule originates from Dr. Max Hooper's research finding that there was a correlation between the number of species in a hedge and its age. It is emphasised that this is not a precise guide but can serve to distinguish hedges planted earlier than Stuart times from those of a later date. Older hedges are more likely to have developed naturally and therefore be of mixed species but also it was customary earlier to plant with more species. The enclosure period saw much planting of hawthorn hedges and the Georgians often included trees in the hedgerow.

The use of hedges as a boundary has a long history; the Romans were familiar with the concept and many hedges existed in Saxon times. Rackham in his book points out that maps of the sixteenth and seventeenth centuries show that much of the ancient countryside was fully hedged (see page 15) and that the majority of those hedges were still existing into the present century. A hedge with two species is often hawthorn with either oak, ash or blackthorn. Colonising is more difficult for some species so if the hawthorn and blackthorn, for instance, are joined by maple and dogwood, then the hedge could date back to the Tudor era. The inclusion of hazel and spindle and six other species could date the hedge as pre-Tudor.

The loss of hedges in East Anglia through modern farming methods is to be lamented and signs that the process is being reversed are welcome. They are a habitat to be preserved for their own beauty and for the wildlife that they harbour. It is known, for example, that butterflies use hedges as a thoroughfare especially so if they lead to a wood. In conclusion, one only has to walk along by a hedge such as that along The Greenway (Walk 7) to appreciate the delights it has in store.

LOCATION MAP OF WALKS WITH STARTING POINTS

1 New Buckenham
2 Loddon
3 Saxlingham
4 Burnham Market
5 Holt
6 Stiffkey
7 Little Walsingham
8 Reepham

9 Weybourn
10 Garboldisham
11 Hingham
12 Mulbarton
13 Thompson
14 Horsey
15 Upton
16 The Raynhams

17 Castle Acre
18 North Creake
19 Narborough
20 Mileham
21 Wiggenhall
22 Castle Rising
23 Marsham
24 Trunch
25 Weeting

THE WALKS - in order of difficulty

Leave livestock, and crops and machinery alone.
Take your litter home.
Help to keep all water clean.
Protect wildlife, plants and trees.
Take special care on country roads.
Make no unnecessary noise.
Enjoy the countryside and respect its life and work.
Guard against all risk of fire.
Fasten all gates.
Keep your dogs under close control.
Keep to public paths across farmland.
Use gates and stiles to cross fences, hedges and walls.

WALK 1: CASTLES AND GREENS
Old and New Buckenham

Start: *New Buckenham. Grid Ref: 088906*
O.S.Map: *Landranger 144.*
Distance: *5 miles*
Time: *3 hours.*
Parking: *Park near St. Martin's Church.*
Refreshments: *The George and Kings Head, New Buckenham.*
  The Ox & Plough, Old Buckenham.

A gentle walk across fields with a short stretch of road taking in two very interesting villages both with attractive cottages and remains of castles.

WALK DOWN THE LANE to the north of St Martins Church passing the graveyard on the right. Go past Hunt's Farm and then take the footpath on the left beside the small electricity sub-station. Cross the stile and aim diagonally across the field to the gate on the left of a small oak. Keep forward on the path towards a small clump of willows that surround what in the winter could be a pond. Cross the plank bridge and go straight forward as far as the lane.

Here turn left and walk to the farm and, opposite another pond, turn right down a broad track.

In about 300 metres turn left (Y.W.M.) and cross the field soon to meet a deep ditch on the left which in late summer is a mass of willow herb, hedge bindweed and knapweed.

The snowy-white flower of Hedge Bindweed, sometimes known as morning glory, is very beautiful and gracious. The blooms will also stay open until late in the evening and even through the night if there is a full moon. The plant is sometimes called convolvulus because of its ability to entwine round its nearest neighbours. It attracts the convolvulus hawk moth which uses its long tongue to extract nectar from the deep trumpet-shaped flowers.

Cross the plank bridge and the stile immediately on the left. Go diagonally across the paddock. Then bear left and in 20 metres turn right through a 'sliding gate' towards the church tower seen ahead. Negotiate a second sliding gate and keep to the right of the churchyard to All Saints Church.

The thatched church has a Norman doorway and an octagonal tower which, inside the church, is round at ground level. There are only three like

45

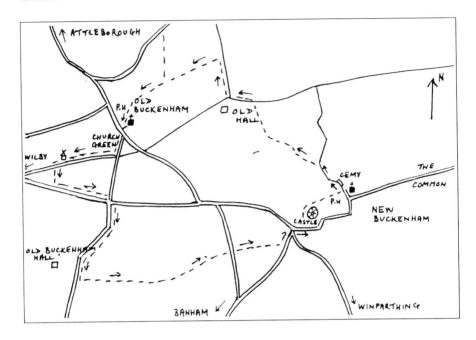

this in Norfolk. The church overlooks the huge green and the little streets around it have some interesting names like Cake Street, Puddledock and Hog's Snout. The castle embankments are the oldest feature of the village and may date from the Roman period. Only the mound remains of the Norman castle which was built inside the earthworks since William D'Albini donated the stone for the building of the nearby priory when he built a new castle at New Buckenham.

Seats near the playground overlooking the common and Ottomer Pond make an ideal place for a picnic.

The walk continues towards the crossroads and the war memorial. Take the road s.p. Wilby and at the next crossroads turn right for Wilby. Go forward past Mill Farm and down Mill Road soon to pass the old mill (now a house). Just past here take the footpath on the left and at the lane turn left. At the next crossroads turn right (s.p. Banham) ignoring the road to New Buckenham. After passing the river, Downmore Farm and the lion-guarded gates to Old Buckenham Hall proceed for another 200 metres and then turn left on to a wide track. Pass through a field and a wild patch of dock to reach a plank bridge. Cross and bear right round the pond and along by the hedge.
Cross the road and the stile, the first of a series that separate two paddocks and

various fields. Arriving at the road turn left and at the crossroads continue forwards towards New Buckenham. In about 500 metres turn down a track by the side of a flint walled barn. The track winds its way round the moat of the ruined castle which is hidden by trees on the far side of the moat. Return to the church ahead.

The sixteenth century Market House

The castle, built in 1138, had the first English example of a round keep. Further enlargements were carried out in the thirteenth century. An order to demolish it was given in 1649. A visit to the ruins may be made by obtaining a key from the Castle Garage. Attractive cottages, early timber fronted and others dating from the nineteenth century, and the polygonal Market House (1559) with its whipping post, make a wander around the village worthwhile. New Buckenham is an example of a planned medieval settlement with streets laid out in a regular pattern radiating from the castle. To the east of the village is the common, one of the largest in Norfolk.

WALK 2: TWO HALLS & A NORMAN CHURCH
Loddon to Hales

Start: *Loddon. Grid Ref: 363988*
O.S.Map: *Landranger 134.*
Distance: *6 miles*
Time: *3 hours.*
Parking: *Car Park by Loddon Church.*
Refreshments: *The Swan or Fox & Hounds, Loddon.*

This walk over gently sloping countryside takes in a Tudor and a Georgian Hall, the former with a magnificent tithe barn, and includes the tiny Norman church at Hales. Note that the route crosses and re-crosses the A46, not a particularly busy road but a fast one, so allow plenty of space before crossing.

LEAVE THE CAR PARK by the main gate to Holy Trinity Church and opposite the entrance porch turn right on a wide 'loke'. At the road turn left and continue forwards to pass the Fox & Hounds. In 100 metres cross the road at the bridge and turn right on to the footpath that runs beside Loddon Beck.

Don't be put off by the industrial complex to the left, the scenery soon improves! Meanwhile the beck and the surrounding banks are the home for several wild flowers. Look out for the spear-shaped leaves of wild arum or their scarlet berries that stand out in the autumn undergrowth. The plant has several local names such as Lords and Ladies, Silly Lovers, and Adam and Eve, all connected with love-making and the name Cuckoo Pint may well have originated from the word cuckold. The roots of the plant, because of their starch content, were used by the Elizabethans for stiffening their pleated ruffs.

The path eventually reaches the A146. Cross with care to the kissing gate or stile seen to the left and continue forward by the side of Warren Hills slopes.

The area could be a set for 'Watership Down' with the pock-marked slopes betraying the presence of many rabbits. Since the earlier centuries when some estates in Norfolk gained income from their rabbit warrens, it is interesting to conjecture whether this particular area had a long history of rabbit farming.

Where the hills end cross the stile on the left and continue in the same direction as before along the left side of the well-established hawthorn hedge.

Blossom in Spring and the berry-laden bushes in the autumn make this a resplendent hedge.

At the metalled lane turn left and in 50 metres bear right towards Hales Hall seen ahead. Pass what could be an old marl pit and at the trees turn left down a wide 'ride'. The path skirts the Hall and then turns left across an open space.

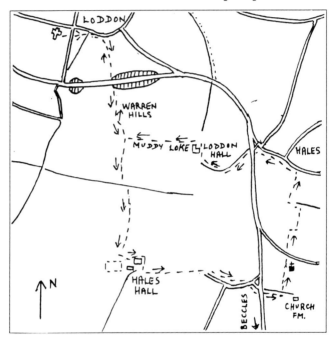

Before turning left it is possible to visit the medieval barn which can be seen to the left of the gateway. This is the largest brick-built barn in Britain, 180 feet long, and dates from c1480. It forms part of the complex of the great house built for Sir James Hobart who was Attorney General in the reign of Henry VII. (A painting of Sir James and his wife hangs in Loddon Church.) There has been a house on the site since before 1086. The present hall was then the Gatehouse and Steward's House, the main hall being on the open ground beyond. Note the narrow slits in the walls of the barn which may indicate that the barn had a defensive purpose as well as being a store-house. At the time of writing there is a plan for the barn to be re-thatched. Behind the barn is a nursery which houses the national collection of citrus fruits as well as many exotic shrubs. This is open to the public Tuesday to Saturday.

49

Norman Doorway, Hales Church.

On leaving the barn the route is across the open space to a lane. (Ignore the track which leads to the right.) Cross the cattle grid and in a short while turn left (s.p. Hales) and at the slipway turn right (s.p. Beccles) and cross the A146. In 20 metres is a gravel track on the left. Follow this as far as a stile and footpath which leads left across the field to Hales Church.

> St Margaret's Church is now classed as redundant and is only used for special occasions, which is a pity for it is a gem. It is a Saxon building dating from the eighth century with a round tower and apse. The Normans added some fine doorways which alone make the visit worthwhile. Unfortunately the church is locked and to obtain the key a further 1½ mile walk is necessary. Nevertheless it is a delightful building and there are some interesting families recorded in the churchyard.

Go out of the church gate and continue forward across the field opposite. Turn right at the hedge and in 20 metres go left between two oaks to continue straight ahead over two fields. Turn left at the track and in about 100 metres turn right along the hedge bearing left at the end as far as a path on the right which heads across a field towards a group of houses. A narrow cut leads to the road.
Here turn left and follow s.p. Loddon, past the Chequered Flag, turning left at the war memorial (s.p. Hales Green). From Green Lane cross the A146 to Green Road and follow this to the cattle grid. Head towards the gates of Loddon Hall, a Georgian mansion, and bear right across Loddon Green between the wall and the cricket pitch. Pass a pond and cross the stile on the left. Follow the path turning left then right on to a wide grassy track between hedges which is known as Muddy Loke. The track later descends to the stile met on the outward route by Warren Hills. From here retrace the route back to Loddon Church.

> The church, which is open from May to October, is well worth a visit. Its Perpendicular style and clerestory make for a beautiful light and cheerful building. It has several interesting features amongst which is a seven sacrament font on steps, the top one being shaped like a Maltese cross. The font was defaced in 1642 by a glazier from Beccles for the sum of six shillings. Look too for the large poor-box.
> Further down the village there are some interesting buildings dating from the eighteenth century.

WALK 3: VILLAGES AND LOST CHURCHES
Saxlingham, Nethergate and Shotesham

Start: *Saxlingham Church. Grid Ref: 232972.*
O.S.Map: *Landranger 134.*
Distance: *6½ miles or 4 miles (shorter version).*
Time: *4 hours or 2 hours (shorter version).*
Parking: *Near Saxlingham Church.*
Refreshments: *Packed lunch advisable.*

A good walk across beautiful, unspoilt countryside. The route passes through two interesting villages and a hamlet providing varied walking by lanes, fields and alongside woods. There are a few short sections of rough walking which, in winter or after wet weather, can be very muddy.

FROM THE CHURCH turn right and walk to the War Memorial. Turn left by the P.O.Stores and proceed up the sandy bridleway. (Ignore the lane to Foxhole). At the crossing of bridleways continue ahead with the high hedge and trees on the left. Where the track bends sharp right take the footpath on the left - look for the finger-post in the hedge - which crosses some rough ground. At the break in the hedge go forward with the hedge now on the right along the edge of the field.

(It looks as though the original footpath runs along the bottom of the hedge-lined ditch but at the time of writing this is somewhat overgrown and blocked here and there. Possibly this section of the path is old and it could be interesting to count the number of different species of tree and shrub in a thirty metre stretch. Hooper's rule, which gives a rough guide to the age of a hedgerow, allows an age of 100 years for each specie so, if there are three different trees and shrubs in the 30m distance, the hedgerow may be 300 years old. See page 41).

At the far corner of the field drop down the bank to find the three way finger-post and turn left. In a short while there is a good view across open countryside. Where the path joins a track turn right and at the road turn right again and continue to Saxlingham Green. Where the road bends bear left, s.p. Shotesham, and, on reaching the telephone box, turn left down Chequers Lane.

In late summer scabious and knapweed grow on the bank. Field Scabious gets its name from its use in the past for curing scabies and other skin diseases. The juice of the plant was either drunk or applied as an ointment. The leaves are food for several kinds of butterflies and moths. In some

52

areas the plant is called 'lady's pin-cushions' or 'pins-and-needles' from the habit of the male stamens standing up erect on the flower head. In the West Country it is called 'bachelor's buttons' after the custom of using the buds to tell a girl which man she should marry. Each bud was given the name of one who was eligible and then she waited to see which developed into the best flower. Strangely, Knapweed is associated with a similar custom. The girl picked the first florets off the flower and tucked the head inside her blouse. If the flower continued to develop then her future husband would soon appear.

Tower of St Mary's, Shotesham and the ruins of St Botolph's.

53

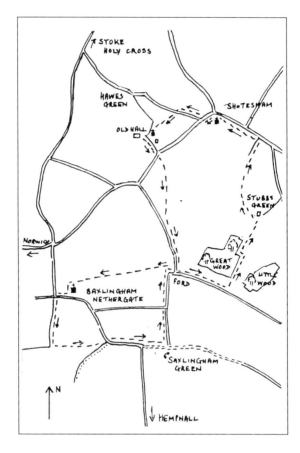

Go past the lane that leads left and continue to the 'S' bend. (At the first bend the shorter version of the walk continues left before reaching the ford. See later below.*)

At the second bend, past the ford, turn right along Wash Lane and in about half a mile look for a footpath that leads across the field on the left to the edge of Great Wood.

After crossing the field the path goes round the edge of the wood crossing a plank bridge over a ditch midway. At the end of the wood follow the trees and hedge round to the left and then cut diagonally across a meadow aiming for a pylon in the distance. At the bottom of the dip a wooden bridge will be seen beyond a hedge. (Don't give up - there is a narrow gap to be found!)

Cross the bridge and go forward up the path to the lane. Turn left to proceed into Shotesham. All Saints Church is reached in half a mile.

The seats near the War Memorial make an ideal spot for a picnic. In springtime the mound is covered in daffodils.

The church is one of four that originally existed in the parish. One, St Mary's, can be seen on the other side of the valley and alongside this is the ruined tower of St Botolph's. The ruins of St Martin's lie just beyond the village. St Mary's and All Saints are still in use and it is possible to obtain keys should they be locked. St Martin's was founded in Saxon times and St Botolph's in 1020 during the reign of King Canute. It later belonged to the Abbot of St Benet and, because he was unpopular with Henry VIII, it fell into a ruin.

St Mary's, to be seen later, was built in 1486. It is interesting that the return for Archbishop Whitgift in 1603 showed that this tiny church had 70 communicants.

Such a group of churches are not an unusual feature of several villages in Norfolk. Indeed some can be even closer to each other as at Reepham. (See Walk 8) Here, the four manors were finally united as a parish in 1731.

At the church turn left down Rogers Lane (s.p. Saxlingham) and in 200 metres turn right along Priory Lane. In a short while take the footpath on the left that heads towards St Mary's Church. The path bears round a small copse surrounding a pond. Continue ahead to cross a narrow lane and, when 20 metres short of the stile, cross the ditch and follow the hedge on the right to the church. Go to the left of the building and then down the farm path past the ruined tower of St Botolph's. (Look for the Colman's Mustard sign).

Cross Rogers Lane and follow the path over the field - in line with the telegraph poles should the footpath have been recently ploughed. At the lane turn left and continue on as far as the ford passed earlier in the walk. Follow the bend round and where the lane straightens take the footpath on the right.

* The footpath sign is fixed to an old gate. Proceed along the left side of the hedge and then over an open space to a wire fence. Cross into a lush meadow and keeping close to the hedge on the left cross a second fence to find the stile a short way further on. The path beyond the stile returns to Saxlingham Church.

The church here has a typical seven sacrament font - Norfolk has 25 out of the 40 that exist in England. During term time, each Thursday after school, there is a service for children from the Primary school. Visiting adults are made very welcome.

WALK 4: BY MARSH AND LANE BETWEEN BURNHAMS
Burnham Market

Start: *Burnham Market. Grid Ref: 832422.*
O.S.Map: *Landranger 132.*
Distance: *9 miles (shorter route 7 miles).*
Time: *4 hours.*
Parking: *Burnham Market Green, nr. St Mary's Westgate.*
Refreshments: *Packed lunch. Tea at The Hoste Arms, The Green, Burnham Market.*

> *The outward half of the walk leads across the marshes to the North Coast Path that borders the broad sweep of the saltings and the distant dunes of the Scolt Head Reserve.*
> *The return is by way of country lane and track bordering farmland.*

LEAVE THE GREEN by way of Herrings Lane between Rose Inn Cottage and Market House 50 metres east of the telephone box. At the end of the houses ignore the track to the left and take the footpath 100 metres further on by the telegraph pole (s.p. Burnham Norton).
At the end of the hedge bear right to the road. Cross the A149 to the lane opposite which leads to Burnham Norton.

A little way along this lane on the left is an impressive Holm Oak tree. Unlike the common oak this is an evergreen with dark green almost black leaves. The bark is brownish-black or black shallowly cracked into squares and the crown of the tree is broad and domed often on many stems. The new leaves unfold in June silvery-white. The upper side soon turns shiny blackish green but the underneath stays dull fawn.

Where the lane bends left take the footpath on the right and then bear left towards the Coastal Path. Turn left at the sea wall. In 2 miles where the wall meets a track (with a wall on both sides a little further on) turn left and go forward up to the A149. Here turn right and in 50 metres go left up the lane by the bus shelter. Here there is a convenient seat for a picnic.
(If an alternative, shorter route back to Burnham Market is desired at this point, retrace steps to the church at Burnham Norton and, a little further along the A149, turn right along the lane s.p. Burnham Market. Continue along this lane for 2 miles to reach the point * below. This saves 2 miles.)
Otherwise continue up the lane and where it bends right by a grove of beech trees

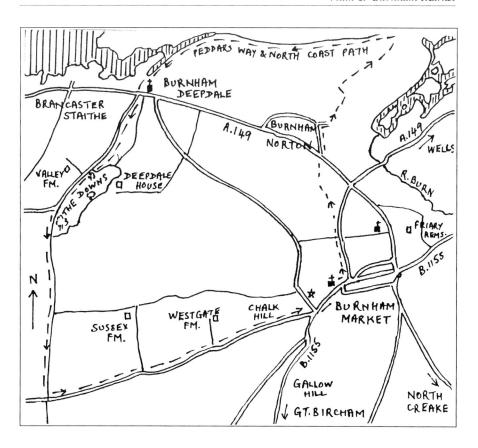

go straight ahead on the stony track. Later ignore the private track to the left and, bearing left at the next junction of tracks, go on ahead to a lane (Ringstead Road). Here turn left. Go past Sussex Farm and later, Westgate Farm, and at the end of Ringstead Road * follow the sign to return to the Green.

Just before the Green is St Mary's Church, Westgate. The tower is unusual with its battlemented parapet decorated with carvings of scenes from the Bible.

Two miles to the south-east is the village of Burnham Thorpe, the birthplace of Horatio Nelson who was the fifth son of the local Rector. The site of the family house is marked by a plaque. The church has memorials to him as well as a lectern made from the timbers of H.M.S. Victory.

WALK 5: ROLLING NORFOLK
Holt to Letheringsett

Start: *Holt. Grid Ref: 078387.*
O.S.Map: *Landranger 133.*
Distance: *5 miles.*
Time: *3 hours.*
Parking: *Kerridge Way Car Park, nr. Budgens Store.*
Refreshments: *Packed lunch or various pubs in Holt.*

A pleasant walk along by wooded countryside and later across a farmland track to the attractive village of Letheringsett and the mill. The return to Holt is across fields.

FROM THE CAR PARK go through the Appleyard site to the Kings Head Inn. After crossing the High Street go down New Street opposite. The lane first passes the cemetery and later the Holt Field Study Centre. Continue ahead past the track to Lawn Farm and a gamekeeper's cottage, The Watering, on the right. Shortly after this take the track that leaves the lane obliquely on the left signed to Bayfield Farm, 'walkers welcome'.

On the way up the track look out for distant views of Blakeney Church.

At the farm veer right to go through the farmyard and at the lane turn left. Continue along the lane keeping forward past the entrance to an Angling Club where a track crosses. At the main road, the A148, cross to Riverside Road, which leads past Letheringsett Mill.

The Mill is open on weekdays and Saturday mornings and there are demonstrations on Tuesday, Wednesday and Thursday afternoons. Further on down the road there are some very attractive cottages, some faced with knapped flints which were often used for decorative work on many local churches. Flint knapping - the craft of breaking flint to make tools or to produce stone with an even surface - was a thriving industry in Brandon on the Suffolk border during the eighteenth century and reached its height during the Napoleonic Wars at the beginning of the following century when one million flints were supplied to the Master General of the Board of Ordnance for the flintlock muskets in use at the time. The invention of the percussion cap adopted by the army in 1838 was virtually the end of an industry which began nearly four thousand years earlier at Grimes Graves. (see Page 34) Obviously, since flints were a widely used material for building in East Anglia, sources near at hand would have been

Cottages with typical knapped flint infill.

used. Architects still occasionally need the skill of knappers to produce a contrasting surface on modern buildings. (For an interesting account of the industry see 'Background to Breckland'.)

On arriving at the ford the route then turns left on to the footpath signed just before the ford.

By the ford, which provided a cooling dip for my dog, Ben, there is a seat which makes it a pleasant spot for a picnic.

A wide track mounts the slope and then turns left at the top of the rise alongside a hedge on the right. The path follows the line of the telegraph poles. Go through a gap in the hedge and continue ahead, crossing two stiles to eventually reach the road (B1110).

Look out for the embankment of a dismantled railway line on the right before the last stile.

At the road turn left to return to Holt. Just before reaching the outskirts turn left by the town sign at the side of the road, drop down the bank to cross the dismantled railway and proceed ahead to the school. Here turn left and then right to return to the car park along Kerridge Way.

Holt is an interesting town with many imposing Georgian houses. The parish church of St Andrews is also worth a visit. The present building, completed early in the fifteenth century is small compared with neighbouring Blakeney and Cley which then were busy ports when Holt was just a small village. Now Holt is the principal town in the area. The church was gutted in the fire of 1708 when most of the village was destroyed. It was re-built in 1727. The rector then, a Dr. Briggs, was able to seek financial help from no less than Viscount Townshend, the owner of Raynham Hall, the Prince of Wales, later George II, and Sir Robert Walpole, who was England's first Prime Minister. (He held the office from 1721-42, was rewarded with an earldom by George II, and also presented with No 10 Downing Street, the future London home of succeeding Prime Ministers.) There is an interesting memorial in the chancel to Edmund Hobart the brother of William who, along with the Rev. Thomas Cooper, a master at Greshams School, was executed on Christmas Day 1650 for their part in a Royalist uprising. They are known as the Holt martyrs. Edmund, who helped promote the revolt, somehow 'efcaped the Malice of the Ufurper. He lived in obfcurity only to die in 1666'.

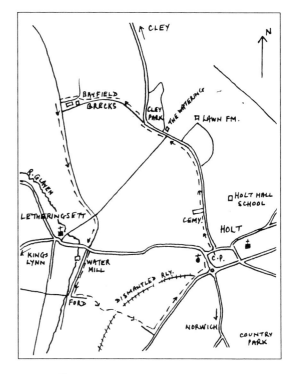

WALK 6: BY FORT AND MARSH
Stiffkey to Warham

Start: *St John's Church, Stiffkey. Grid Ref: 974430*
O.S.Map: *Landranger 132.*
Distance: *6 miles. (7¼ with detour to fort).*
Time: *3 hours.*
Parking: *By the church.*
Refreshments: *The Three Horseshoes, Warham*

> *A pleasant , easy walk with splendid views across country for the first half,*
> *returning along the marshes by Peddars Way and the North Norfolk Coast Path.*
> *The detour to the fort is well worthwhile but can be made by car later if desired.*

STARTING FROM St John's Church turn left to go through the village. Take extreme care to begin with since the road is narrow with blind corners. In about 300 metres turn left on to the road s.p. Cockthorpe. Later bear right s.p. Binham and Warham.

Alexanders grows profusely along the bank here. At the top of the rise there are extensive views to the west beyond Wells.

Continue on ahead and, just past the ford, at the crossroads turn right.

In the autumn, along the verge on the right, Scabious and Toadflax are to be found. In the summer the yellow and orange flowers of Common Toadflax are distinctive, the narrow leaves being similar to flax - hence its name. 'Toad' may have been applied because it was useless unlike flax. Squeeze the side of the flower and the mouth opens and this has given rise to various other names for the plant such as lion's mouth, pig's chops and devil's head.

The Three Horseshoes is soon reached and a welcome break can be made.

All Saints Church opposite has an unusual memorial to one of its rectors, the Rev. Henry Cattell who, in 1900, was captain of the English Rugby Football Team. He later served as Chaplain to the Allied forces at Gallipoli in 1915.

To visit the fort turn left at the crossroads opposite the pub and in about half a mile turn right on to a footpath which leads in 300 metres straight to the fort.

The fort to the south of Warham is most impressive. A large, circular area of ground 150 paces in diameter is ringed by a double rampart which rises to thirty feet above the intervening ditch. North-west Norfolk was the centre for the Iceni tribe in pre-Roman times and this is one of several defensive forts that were constructed between 100-50 B.C. The ramparts would have had a wooden stockade and the central area was large enough to accommodate a considerable number of people and their livestock who would have retreated there when there was danger of attack.

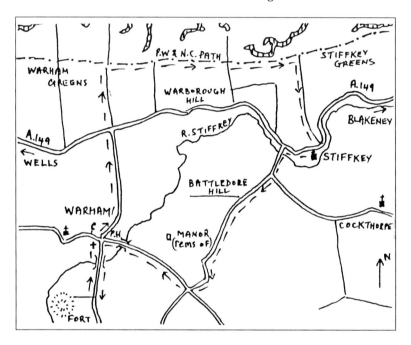

Return to the crossroads to continue the walk along the lane by the side of The Three Horseshoes to arrive at the A149 in one mile. Cross straight over to the track which leads towards the marshes. At the metal gate turn right on to the Coast Path.

By the side of the 'hard' leading towards the sea it is possible to find samphire growing. It was at this point that we met an old lady who over the years had come here to pick the fleshy green shoots known as 'poor man's asparagus'. The season for the plant lasts, she told us, from late June to August. You may still find it in the Autumn but by then it is too tough to eat. We were informed that it is best cooked for about 20 minutes with a very small amount of salt. It can also be pickled. Marsh Samphire is also known as Perennial Glasswort. The glassworts get their name from the fact that they were once used in the manufacture of glass. The fleshy stems were gathered, dried and burned in large quantities. The resulting ash which was high in soda was then fused with sand to make what today would be a poor quality glass.

Warham fort ramparts.

Continue along the Coast Path which, after passing a N.T. sign marking the boundary of Stiffkey Marshes, wends along the edge of a gully or channel wide enough for a boat. In about 200 metres turn right up a track by a second N.T. sign and keep straight ahead to meet the road. Here turn right to return to the church.

WALK 7: ALONG THE PILGRIM'S WAY
Little Walsingham to Great Snoring

Start: *Little Walsingham. Grid Ref: 934369.*
O.S.Map: *Landranger 132.*
Distance: *4¼ miles.*
Time: *2 hours.*
Parking: *Car Park at the top of Common Place opposite the Shrine Bookshop.*
Refreshments: *The Black Lion and other Pubs and Cafes in Walsingham.*

This is a very enjoyable walk with lots of interest and superb views to the coast and across country. The return from Great Snoring is by The Greenway, a delightful ancient track.

ON LEAVING the car park cross Common Place passing the Bull Inn on the right to descend the hill past the Shrine. Ignore the turn to Wighton and continue up the rise to the crossroads. Here turn right into Church Street and walk as far as All Saints Church. Just before the church wall turn left up the concrete road leading to Abbey Farm.

The church is well worth a visit either now or later in a wander around Walsingham. The church was gutted by fire in 1961 and was later restored to become a very light and cheerful building. Here is one of the finest seven sacrament fonts in the country.

One interesting memorial is to Sir Henry Sydney, a cousin of Sir Philip Sydney who commanded an English army in the Netherlands during the reign of Elizabeth I.

So that the army's supplies should not go astray he ordered that they should all be marked with a broad arrow. (The family coat of arms has a similar arrow in the top left corner) Since that time the Government has ordered that all its property should also be marked with the arrow.

The Sydney family occupied the Manor of Walsingham from 1538-1638.

A few paces up the road turn left on to the footpath that leads diagonally across the field heading towards a cleft between banks to the right of a line of trees. Cross the stile into a second meadow and aim for a stile in the far corner to the right of a clump of seven chestnut trees. At the lane turn left and at the next junction turn right s.p. Thursford.

This part of the walk was alive with pheasants on my visit. At the top of the next rise there are wonderful views to the coast.

A little further on is Hill House Farm. Here take the footpath opposite keeping the hedge on the left. The path soon crosses to the other side of the hedge and Great Snoring Church can be seen ahead. The path then turns left for 80 metres after which go right towards the church, this time with the hedge on the left. Arriving at Top farm bear left to go round some green silos and head to the left of a row of cupressus to gain the lane by a cottage. From here turn right and continue ahead over the crossroads s.p. East Barsham. Opposite the lane to Fakenham turn right on to The Greenway to Walsingham.

Common Place with brick pump house, Walsingham.

The different species of tree and shrub lining the Greenway indicate that this is a very old track. Did autumn crab apples litter the ground in the Middle Ages? What stories can the trees tell? This is a good path on which to test Hooper's Rule (see Walk 3).

Keep on the Greenway all the way to the road which is reached after passing between woods, ignoring a track which goes right. Turn right at the road and again at the next junction to return to Walsingham passing the ruins of the Friary on the way.

Little Walsingham has a place in history as a centre of pilgrimage since 1061 when a Lady Richeld had a vision telling her to build a replica of Mary and Joseph's house in Nazareth.

The resulting shrine attracted thousands of pilgrims in the Middle Ages including both Henry III and Edward I. The shrine, a Priory and the Franciscan Friary were all destroyed during the Reformation. The shrine was rebuilt in the 1930s and since then the village is regularly thronged with pilgrims.

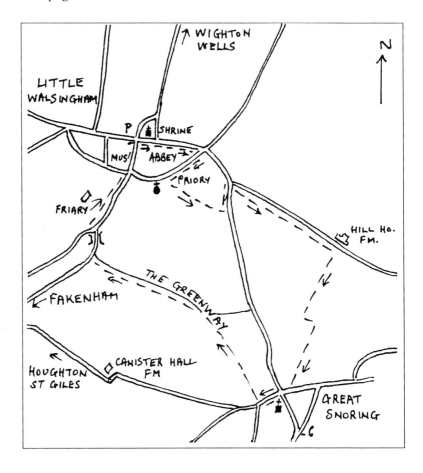

WALK 8: RAILWAY NOSTALGIA
Reepham to Themelthorpe

Start: *Near Reepham. Grid Ref: 091216.*
O.S.Map: *Landranger 133.*
Distance: *7 miles.*
Time: *3 hours.*
Parking: *Park near the railway bridge 1m south of Reepham on the road between Reepham and Sparham down the turning to Bawdeswell.*
Refreshments: *Crown Inn, Reepham or packed lunch.*

> *Of special interest to railway historians but a delightful walk in its own right with unexpected vistas after emerging from the trees or a cutting. The walk is almost entirely along the line of the old railway known as the Themelthorpe Link. Because of the undisturbed nature of the surroundings the line has developed into a haven for wildlife.*

WALK BACK TO the Reepham side of the bridge. Immediately after going under the bridge turn left up a track and in 50 metres turn left by a fingerpost and double back up the slope of the embankment on to Marriott's Way. Turn right to proceed along the embankment.

Ash, hawthorn and oak appear to be the main trees bordering the line with the occasional sycamore. The embankment soon levels out to open up views of the surrounding countryside before entering a cutting.

At the road (B1145) go straight over.

This was almost certainly the site of a level crossing - note how the road has been built up on either side.
A further cutting and two bridges over narrow lanes and a railway worker's hut are other signs along the way of its former use until the line crosses the lane at Themelthorpe. The cottage at the side of the first gate was probably that of a railwayman. Note the stretch of embankment beyond the cottage to the right and the bridge almost hidden by the trees. Two railways crossed here. The embankment was cut away to form the Themelthorpe curve which was opened in 1960.
The curve linked two lines, the M.& G.N. line between Themelthorpe and Norwich and the Great Eastern line between Themelthorpe and Aylsham. Both lines, largely used for transport of livestock, grain and beet, had become uneconomic. The link was opened for the transport of concrete

products from Lenwade to Norwich and was closed in 1985 when production ceased. The Way is named after William Marriott who was the Chief
Engineer of M.& G.N.

**Cross the lane and the gate opposite and continue to follow the route of the line to
the right.**

The next part is more shaded and damp and a variety of fungi can be seen
in season. Later, a bridge over the railway still betrays the brackets that
held the communication system.
A stream crosses underneath the line further on, a minor tributary of the
River Wensum. Later at the end of a 'tunnel of trees' Old Hall farm is seen
on the left, a lake on the right and then Salle Church tower to the left.

**Where a lane meets the line on the left look for steps that descend the embankment.
Go down to the lane and under the bridge bearing left at the fork in the road. Keep
forward to the road (B1145).**

Before leaving the B1145 it is possible to visit the old Reepham Station a few
metres to the left.

**Otherwise turn left and immediately cross the road to Station Plain opposite and
then veer right by the Crown Inn along Ollands Road. Keep ahead and then turn**

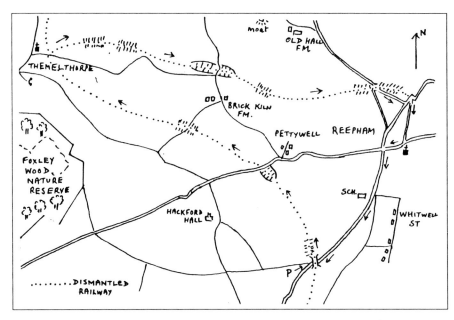

68

right into Church Street past a thatched cottage and St Mary and St Michael's Churches.
Cross the village square with its Georgian houses and at the crossroads turn left down School Road past the Fire Station and the Cemetery to return to the start about ¾ mile ahead.

The reason for the two churches in Reepham being so close to one another is interesting. (See page 26).

In the fifteenth century there were three Reepham churches all sharing the same graveyard. A cross marked the point where the three parish boundaries met.

The idea that two sisters each bequeathed a church in rivalry is legendary and occurs in other places in the country.

St Mary's, Reepham is now the principal church of worship. St Michael's, Whitwell is used mainly as a church hall. All Saints, Hackford was destroyed by fire in 1543. Its tower was demolished in 1796.

WALK 9: ALL KINDS OF COUNTRY
Weybourne to Kelling Heath

Start: *Weybourne. Grid Ref: 110438.*
O.S.Map: *Landranger 133.*
Distance: *5½ miles.*
Time: *2½ hours.*
Parking: *Car Park on the coast.*
Refreshments: *Packed lunch.*

> *This is an excellent walk notable for its grand views and varied countryside. First a walk alongside the shingle beach, then a stretch of marshland, an ascent to heathland and a return through woodland, each with their own diverse wildlife.*

FROM THE CAR PARK mount the steps to the shingle, turn left and, keeping close to the fence, follow the path on the landward side of the shingle bank. Where the fence ends at Kelling Hard, turn left up the track which is soon bordered on both sides by barbed wire fences.

> There are views of Salthouse and Blakeney Church to the right.

The path later passes two wooden farm gates giving access to The Quags, a bird reserve, on the right and there is water on the left which provides a resting place for waders and wildfowl. At the 'T' junction of paths turn left and continue to the road. (A149) Here turn left past Seaview Cottage and in 300 metres turn right on to a footpath. Keep on ahead up the grassy path ignoring the opening on the left.

> The path narrows and becomes quite sandy. At first it is bordered by bracken and later ash trees and higher up by birch. Higher still the undergrowth becomes gorse, heather and birch scrub.

At the top take the second of the two paths on the right (diagram). Go forward and on arriving at the road cross to the path opposite. Continue up to the railway cottage and cross the railway with care. (Trains!) Immediately turn left and follow the path along by the railway fence.

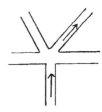

Later on there is a superb view of Weybourne and its Mill. Where the path widens bear right through the gorse bushes as far as the bench seat - a pleasant spot for a picnic. Then turn left down a wide grassy path to a second bench below the railway

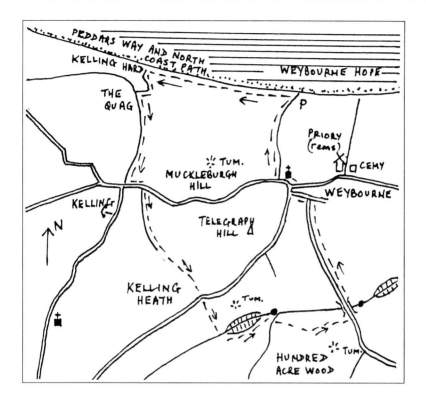

embankment. Now bear right and then keep left to go through the wood beside the railway. At Kelling Halt continue on the path bearing away from the halt to join a wide track, later passing a pond on the right.

Carry on along the path near the railway and later, keeping a water filled hollow on the left, go between barbed wire fences to a driveway and thence to the road. Turn left down Sandy Hill Lane past Weybourne Station. Turn right at the 'give way' sign in the village into Church lane and at the church turn left. In a few metres turn right to return to the car park in just under half a mile.

WALK 10: FARM AND FOREST
Garboldisham

Start: *Garboldisham Church. Grid Ref: 004816.*
O.S.Map: *Landranger 144.*
Distance: *7½ miles.*
Time: *3½ hours.*
Parking: *At the Village Hall opposite the church.*
Refreshments: *The Fox, Garboldisham or packed lunch.*

A bracing walk across fields and alongside forest with a stretch of quiet road between. Extensive views across open country add to the enjoyment of the walk.

FROM THE CHURCH return past the Old Shoemaker's House to the Fox public house. Turn left and go past Water Lane as far as The Old Rectory, a large house on the right. Take the footpath which leaves the road at the side of the Rectory drive. At the end of the narrow path, turn left, ignore the bridleway and bear left to the road ahead. At the road turn right and continue as far as the next junction. Here, go left to pass Ling Farm which is surrounded by majestic beech trees. Keep on ahead to the bend in the lane and take the path which leaves the lane on the left to go behind farm buildings and across fields. A little further on the path becomes bordered by a ditch on either side.
[The next stretch can be tricky and possibly muddy and you may wish to continue on to the road, the B1114, and then turn right to regain the route further on. See *]

Where the ditch begins turn right alongside a ditch between the fields keeping the ditch on the left. Go forward across two fields, skirting a small depression in between, and at the hedge and a cluster of poplar trees, turn right and in a few metres turn left at the gap to gates on either side of a small stream. (This could be dry in summer). Cross the stream and immediately after the second gate turn left towards the gate at the far end of the field beside a copse. Keep the copse on the right to reach the B1114 by a green, metal farm gate.

* Turn right and continue along the road to take the first junction which goes obliquely left. (Do not go as far as the crossroads). Keep on this road for one and a half miles until you arrive at the point where five roads meet. At this junction ignore the road returning to Garboldisham and take the second exit, the road alongside the forest.

Here it is time to indulge in some historical fantasy! Imagine the noise of a Roman legion marching, for this is a Roman road, one of a network that helped to link the southern garrisons with the forts on the Norfolk coast.

Now look out for a footpath which leaves the road on the left not far from the junction and about 30 metres past the first barred gate to the forest. The path edges along on the left of the trees gradually veering away from the road to eventually meet the Devil's Ditch, an earthwork which continues across Garboldisham heath.

Although the bank has disappeared in parts the Ditch can still be seen and the bank is now topped with hawthorn and scrub. The Ditch is a Saxon earthwork, obviously once much higher, and is thought to have been planned to block the Roman road, now the A1066.

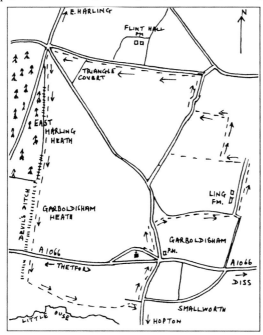

Go along by the Ditch as far as the main road, the A1066. Cross straight over and descend the bank to continue along by the left side of the hedge. Follow the line of trees round to the left and at the fence cross the stile seen to the left. Carry on along by the trees on the right aiming in a short while for a small barn seen ahead. After passing the barn go towards the stile in the left corner of the field about 50 metres to the left of the stream. Cross and continue forward with the hedge on the right. The path then enters a copse. At the track veer right to gain the road.

Garboldisham Mill is about 400 metres to the right and it may be viewed on Wednesdays and Fridays between 9 am and 1 pm.

Otherwise turn left and return to Garboldisham village.

73

WALK 11:   A GEORGIAN VILLAGE
Hingham

Start: *Hingham. Grid Ref: 022022.*
O.S.Map: *Landranger 144.*
Distance: *5 miles.*
Time: *2½ hours.*
Parking: *The Fairland, an open space opposite the church.*
Refreshments: *The White Hart. Teashop on Fairland.*

A pleasant walk across countryside with only two short stretches of quiet lanes.
Hingham, once a country retreat for Georgian gentry, is a most attractive village
and well worth an hour's exploration.
The walk starts from The Fairland, an open space where three fairs for livestock
and pleasure were held annually until 1882.

FROM THE CHURCH cross The Fairland and turn right down the lane marked by
'no entry' signs. The name, Pottle's Alley, is posted at the far end. Then turn left
and immediately right down Hardingham Street.

Before turning right look behind for the house with Dutch gables, an
example of many to be found in Norfolk. The use of pantiles for roofing
became widespread after the seventeenth century. The Dutch gable also
became more common about this time. Raising the gable above the level
of the roof line was a way of preventing the tiles being lifted by strong
winds - something which had not been a great problem with a thatched
roof. The cottage next door but one is the only thatched one in the centre
of the village.

In about 60 metres turn left down Folly Lane. After passing some allotments the
path continues at first on the left side of a ditch, later to switch to the right.

Remnants of snow still lay in the ditches but a cloudless sky had encouraged the larks to rise and sing and there were several hares to be seen on
the open fields to the right the first day I walked across here. The brown
hare is common all over Great Britain wherever there is cultivation. Its
greater size distinguishes it from the rabbit as does its black tips and tail.
Their colour in winter is sometimes greyer than the brown colours of
summer. They feed mainly at night and lie up in their 'forms' by day.
Although hares can destroy crops they are not such a pest as rabbits since
they rarely associate in great numbers. Unlike the rabbit they are native to
this country. The blue hare is restricted to Scotland.

In a short while the path passes a pond on the left and then bears right along by a hedge before turning left along a track that runs in front of poultry houses. Passing the front of these turn right to find the path on the left that crosses a plank bridge and leads towards the next farm.

At the next hedge turn left towards the lane. Ignore the plank and rope bridge across the ditch on the right. At the road turn right to pass first Browne's Farm and then Manson Green Farm and then take the track that leaves the lane at the side of a bungalow on the right.

*Hardingham
Church*

Early in the year look for aconites and snowdrops in the gateway to Manson Green Farmhouse. The latter used to be known as 'the fair maid of February', a reference to the custom of village girls wearing a bunch of snowdrops as a sign of purity on the Feast of Purification of St Mary.

Where the track bends right veer left and proceed forward as far as a track which crosses at right angles; here turn left beside a conifer copse. At the lane turn right and continue along as far as Hardingham Church.

75

Turn right almost opposite the path up to the church and follow the path that leaves diagonally left alongside the steep sided ditch. Continue by the ditch as far as the lane. Here ignore the footpath opposite and turn right along the lane. At Nordelph Corner where the lane curves left continue forward on the path ahead to meet a track leading to a house. Bear right on the path that leads round the house and then along the hedge. A tall, tree-lined hedge and ditch soon crosses at right angles and here turn left keeping the hedge on the left. Hardingham Church is now immediately in line behind and Hingham Church may be seen ahead.

In a short while cross the stile, turn right and, after crossing another stile, look for a gap in the hedge about 100 metres further on. Here turn left. (Do not go as far as the wooden farm gate.) Go on ahead with the hedge on the right and in about 300 metres bear left.

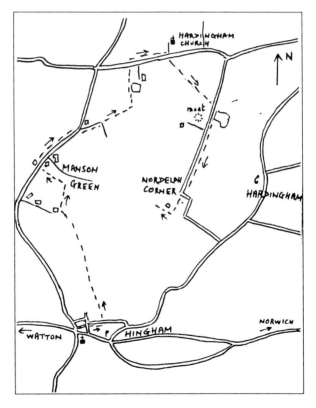

Soon you must look out for the waymark sign in the hedge on the right and a plank bridge over the ditch. Cross here and look for the path that leads across the field towards a white house diagonally opposite. (Depending upon the time of year the path may have been ploughed.) Head towards the house and, at the corner go right along the path that edges round two fields towards the playing field of Hingham School. Cross the stile and turn left alongside the school building. At Hardingham Street, turn right to return to The Fairland.

Hingham is mentioned as Hincham Regis in Domesday which shows that the village was once part of the King's estate. Indeed, in St Andrew's Church records show that this was from 925 - c1150 and then the Lordship of the Manor was granted to a Henry de Rye, Baron of Rye. The Lordship was then handed on over the next few centuries. Thomas, Lord Morley was Lord of the Manor in the fifteenth century and he is commemorated by a magnificent tomb in red stone, ('one of the most impressive 15th century wall monuments in England'. Pevsner).

Another interesting memorial in the church is to Samuel Lincoln who was one of a number of people from Hingham who emigrated to America in 1637 to seek religious freedom. He was an ancestor of Abraham Lincoln and the memorial has been provided by Americans.

Look too for the Winchester Bushel Measure, another connection with the U.S.A. since the bushel is still used there as a standard measure. The measure in the church is one of only a few that exist and was provided by the Lord of the Manor following an Act of Parliament in 1670. The bushel was a standard measure in this country from 800 to 1824.

An excellent, short guide to the village by Roger Norris is available in the church.

77

WALK 12: TWO VILLAGES NEAR NORWICH
Mulbarton and Swardeston

Start: *Mulbarton. Grid Ref: 195012.*
O.S.Map: *Landranger 134.*
Distance: *6 miles.*
Time: *2 hours.*
Parking: *Near Mulbarton Church.*
Refreshments: *Packed lunch. A welcome seat overlooks the green at Mulbarton.*

A very pleasant walk, with only a short stretch along a metalled lane, from the edge of Mulbarton to the village of Swardeston. The return is along the valley of the River Tas, a promising area for wildlife.

TAKE THE FOOTPATH that leaves the churchyard opposite the church porch. After crossing the stile continue forward away from the church bearing right to go round a farm building on to a track. At the next building pass through a metal gate clearly marked with footpath rules keeping ahead on a wide straight track lined by a hedge on the right. Veer right again where the track curves and continue in the same direction passing a copse on the right.
At the lane turn left and keep on this lane as far as the B1113 passing first a wood on the left and Cowthorpe Manor on the right.

An imposing brick built barn with stepped gables dominates the farm buildings.

At the B1113 go straight across and down Short Lane and turn right at the junction. In about 100 metres turn left on a path which leaves the lane just short of Cavell House. A magnificent beech tree stands in front of the house.

Edith Louisa Cavell (1865 - 1915), a nurse, was the second daughter of the rector of Swardeston. In 1907 she became matron of a medical Institute in Brussels which became a Red Cross Hospital during World War I. In August 1915 she was arrested by the Germans and charged with helping over 200 Allied soldiers to escape to Holland. During her trial she did not deny the charges and was later shot.

A path, sometimes muddy, leads through thickets to the common. Follow the edge of the wood to the right and then aim across the space towards the last house at the bottom of the slope. Just before the bridge over the stream take the footpath on the left. Do not enter the first field but cross the stile beforehand on the right and then

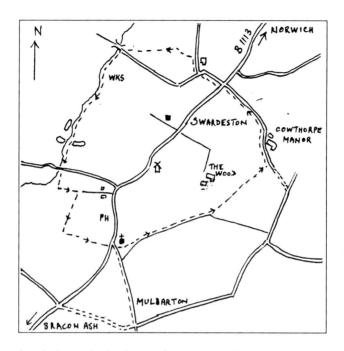

carry on ahead along the hedge. After passing the Water Works, Swardeston Church tower may be seen behind the trees to the left. At the copse go up the bank to the stile and turn right. Keep ahead alongside scrub land and then through trees and across an open patch. The path wends between ponds, crosses a small sluice (Care!), and then passes a small plantation (at the time of writing the trees were 12 - 15 feet tall).

Pass through a gate in a fence, cross the lane and continue forward and up a bank. Go up the left side of the field, turn right at the top to cross an open gap marked by three trees. Cross another field, negotiate the highstile and go diagonally over the paddock to another high stile. Turn left to reach the road and again left to return across the common to the church.

The common is one of the largest in Norfolk extending over 50 acres. There was a move to enclose the common in 1865 but great opposition thwarted the attempt.

WALK 13: THE GREAT EASTERN PINGO TRAIL
Cranberry Rough and Thompson Common

Start: *A1075 near Stow Bedon. Grid Ref: 940967.*
O.S.Map: *Landranger 144.*
Distance: *7½ miles.*
Time: *3 hours.*
Parking: *N.N.T. car park on right side of A1075 from Watton.*
Refreshments: *Packed lunch.*

> *A superb walk first along the site of an old railway line wending through woods rich in bird and insect life to Hockham Heath, along part of Peddars Way, and concluding with a trail across Thompson Common and a wander around the pingos.*
> *The trail is well signed. Yellow and green discs with the name of the trail around the edge make directions almost unnecessary.*

WALK SOUTH away from the road along a path lined by pussy willows to cross duckboarding by the side of farm buildings. The path wends between birch woods with numerous pingos being a feature. The track then becomes lined with hawthorn and soon passes Crossing Keeper's Cottage of which little is left except the barest foundations.

The track has followed the line of a Great Eastern Railway junction line between Roudham and Swaffham which linked the line between Thetford and Norwich to places such as Watton and Pickenham. This branch line, known locally as 'The Crab and Winkle', opened in 1865 and was finally closed in 1965.

In a short while look out for the circular logo by a stile (do not follow the track which bears right across open fields). The path then enters Cranberry Rough.

Rough certainly it is - a swamp woodland which shows signs of past coppicing, the majority of trees standing in peaty black pools of water interspersed with tufts of thick tussock sedge. The area developed on the site of a former lake and is an important breeding ground for several species of duck such as shoveler and gadwall. It is a strange scene - perhaps Norfolk's version of a mangrove!

The path then crosses more open pine forest to enter a cutting with the old Great Eastern fence still standing strong either side of the embankment. At the end of

Cranbrry Rough

the cutting climb the steps on the right and skirt the spruce wood to reach a lane. Turn right here and at the fork bear right on to Peddars Way passing between woods dotted here and there with some old gnarled chestnut and beech trees. The gravel track then crosses an open space.

Between the old railway and here is a good area for spotting deer. During my first walk along here both fallow and muntjac were to be seen. Both belong to the Artiodactyla order or even-toed ungulates which include sheep, goats and pigs. Red and Roe deer are the only species native to this country. The Fallow is a native of southern Europe and may have been

81

introduced by the Romans although this is by no means certain. It stands about three feet in height and is reddish-fawn or 'fallow'. In summer they are dappled with white spots and after October they became greyish-brown without spots. The white rump, or speculum, is noticeable.

The Chinese Muntjac is smaller, about half the height of the Fallow, and chestnut red with grey speckles and a white throat. Their antlers are only a few centimetres long but their upper canines, or tusks, could be used when fighting. They resemble a large dog and indeed they do bark when alarmed or during the rutting season. Both Fallow and Muntjac exist in a feral state although they are favoured for parks.

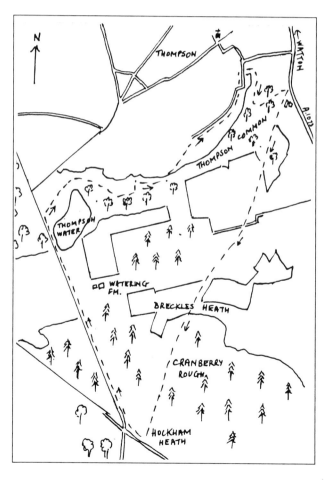

Do not turn right at the track marked 89 but continue forward on Peddars Way past the sign to Watering Farm and, in a short while, past Thompson Water, a man-made lake on the right.

It is a shallow lake formed from the damming of a river in 1845 and is an important breeding and wintering site for wildfowl.

Shortly after this turn right on to the path across Thompson Common marked by a N.N.T. sign. Follow the path to the left soon to pass a large birch log which makes a convenient seat for a break.

Continue on this path to a broad bridge over a stream and, after crossing, turn immediately left to follow the stream. Later the path crosses open fields to join a lane. Go past stables, several cottages and over a bridge before rejoining the trail path that leaves the lane to enter woods on the right.

The pingos soon become obvious as the trail winds between a series of round ponds of varying sizes each surrounded by a bank. Very common on the eastern edge of the Fens and in Breckland, they were often concentrated in large numbers, sometimes as many as a hundred to a square mile. They are the remnants of pingos formed over 20,000 years ago during the last ice age. Water below the surface froze to form mounds of ice which pushed up the ground in the same way that frozen cream forces off the milk bottle cap. During summer thaws the surface soil and meltwater ran off the slope to form the surrounding bank. The ice finally melted to form the depressions we see today.

The word 'pingo' comes from the Eskimo since similar formations occur in Alaska and Greenland. Snipe and lapwing are known to breed on the pingos and they are home for plants such as bogbean and water violet and for rare dragonflies and butterflies.

The path winds between the pingos to return through woods to the car park.

WALK 14: WINDPUMPS AND DUNES
Around Horsey to the Sea

Start: *Horsey Windpump. Grid Ref: 457223.*
O.S.Map: *Landranger 134.*
Distance: *3 miles or 5 miles.*
Time: *1½ or 2½ hours.*
Parking: *National Trust Car Park.*
Refreshments: *Tea Shop or Nelson Head Inn.*

The shorter version of this walk is an opportunity for a gentle stroll first skirting the edge of Horsey Mere and then along the edge of a dyke to a ruined windpump. The return is by field and lane with the opportunity of visiting Horsey Church. The longer walk includes a stretch of the coast between two gaps in the dunes.

FROM THE CAR PARK go up the steps and turn right along the towpath beside the staithe. The path veers right along the edge of the mere and a boardwalk leads to a stile. Go diagonally across the field to a second stile. A windpump may be seen ahead.

The area is part of the Horsey Estate and the owners have thoughtfully provided signs (a white circle on a black background) to indicate the route.

The path goes between reeds to another boardwalk that leads to a Cut. Continue along this as far as the ruined windpump.
Then turn right across the field beside a dyke. The path bears left and across a bridge over the dyke to head towards some houses.
At the lane it's decision time! Turn right for the shorter walk and left for the longer one. Directions for this continue below**.

For the shorter version turn right and immediately left and continue forward with a hedge on the left. The path bears right round the field and then beside a few houses to arrive at Horsey Church.

All Saints Church, memorable for its unalloyed simplicity and its tranquil setting, is well worth a visit. The tower and the core of the nave and chancel were built before 1066 and may well date back to the 900s. The round tower, one of 119 in Norfolk, is capped by an octagonal belfry added in the fifteenth century which was when other additions to the church such as the porch and many of the windows were made. Being on the Norfolk Broads it is fitting that the church is thatched.

84

From the church bear left past the playing field, then right to follow the B1159 back to Horsey Windpump.

The windpump is a drainage mill and was built by a famous Ludham millwright, Dan England in 1912. The previous mill had stood for 200 years and was known as Horsey Black Mill since, like many mills, it was tarred to keep out the weather. The top of the old mill had blown off in a gale and the new structure built of bricks made in Martham, rests on the old foundations. The purpose of windpumps was to pump water from the dykes into the higher system of Broads and waterways. The Horsey pump worked until 1943 and like others had an auxiliary steam pump (later converted to diesel) hence the accompanying pump house. There is a good view from the top of the mill which is open from the end of March to the end of September.

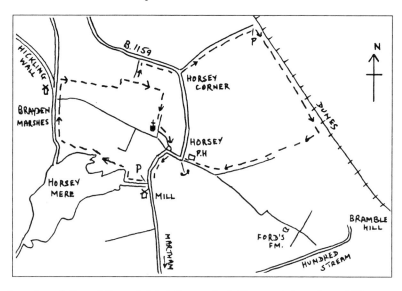

** At the lane turn left and then right at the road. At the next sharp bend, Horsey Corner, turn left down a white gravel track to re-enter the Horsey estate. At the car park either take the path right on the landward side of the dunes or, if preferred, go right along the beach. At the next concrete gap in the dunes (about 15 minutes walk, or more if on the beach!) turn right on a wide track fenced both sides. This eventually meets a metalled lane and after a short stretch it is possible during the summer months to turn left across fields (a non-dedicated right of way) to return to the start point. Otherwise continue on past the Nelson Head and bear left along the road at the telephone box.

85

The area of Horsey, or Horse Island, was once called 'Devil's Country' owing to its wild nature. The area has always suffered from flooding. In 1784 the Curate of the church recorded that on several occasions he narrowly escaped drowning on his way to conduct worship. In 1938 severe flooding left only 100 acres above water which took four months to drain and it was a further five years before the land was once more suitable for farming. Severe floods again occurred in 1953. New sea defences were constructed in 1988.

The population of the village has remained just under 100 for many, many years.

Windpump on the Broads at Horsey

WALK 15: DYKES AND RIVERS
Upton and the River Bure

Start: *Upton Dyke. Grid Ref: 402128.*
O.S.Map: *Landranger 134.*
Distance: *7½ miles.*
Time: *4 hours.*
Parking: *Staithe Car Park. (From the crossroads in Upton down Chapel Lane and Back Road.).*
Refreshments: *The White Horse in Upton Village, or a packed lunch.*

A wonderful walk which on a fine sunny day should be done at a leisurely pace to enjoy the beauty of the area. The first part of the walk stretches along the River Bure between Upton and South Walsham and then returns by field, woodland and lane.

FROM THE CAR PARK take the path on the left of Upton Dyke alongside the moored boats. At the end of the dyke continue left for nearly five miles alongside the River Bure.

There is plenty of birdlife along the river. Look out for kingfishers especially near the first Cut on the far bank where holes in the bank may well be their nests. Great Crested Grebes, with their long necks, pointed bills and ear-tufts, frequently dive under the water. Greylag geese are common on the water too and herons may well be disturbed from the bank. During the summer, apart from the ever-churring Reed warblers, Reed Buntings are common. The latter can be seen flicking their tails as they cling to the reeds along the banks of the river and dykes. The male is conspicuous with its black head and collar and white throat, whilst the female has a brown head. Its flight is jerky and white outer tail feathers become obvious.

The route passes two old windpumps beside the bank at one of which it is possible to see the old diesel engine which superseded wind power and later there is a modern alternative complete with its own digger to extract debris from the dyke. About halfway along this section of the walk the Bure is joined by the River Thurne, the confluence overlooked by two more windpumps. Later, on the far bank are the ruins of St Benet's Abbey.

St Benet's Abbey is now in the jurisdiction of the Bishop of Norwich who has the distinction of being the only 'Abbot/Bishop' in the House of Lords.

Each year on the first Sunday in August he conducts an open-air service by the ruins having sailed along the Bure in a wherry.

The Abbey is thought to have been founded in 1020 on land granted by King Canute. By the end of the thirteenth century St Benet's owned property in 76 Norfolk parishes. Much profit had been made from the sale of peat turves (see page 19).

The abbey escaped dissolution under Henry VIII but the last monk left in 1545.

The nearby cross of oak from the Sandringham estate was erected in 1987.

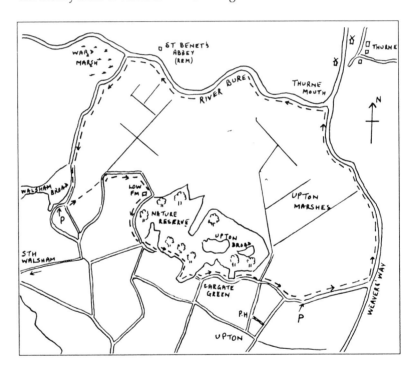

In a short while the path turns away from the Bure and follows the Fleet dyke to South Walsham Broad. At the Broad sign continue past the toilets and the boatyards. By Staitheside look out for the private mooring and a very convenient bench for lunch overlooking a superb view of South Walsham Broad, possibly one of the most beautiful of the Broads.

Arriving at the metalled lane bear left and in 20 metres take the footpath left across the fields. At the next lane turn left and in 200 metres turn right on to a grassy path signed with the Broads green arrow. Continue forward past some farm buildings

St Benet's Abbey ruins from the River Bure.

and bear left at the lane to go past the entrance to the Upton Fen Nature Reserve. At the crossroads go left (signed again with the Broads arrow) along the lane edged at the beginning with five white posts.

At the end of the farmyard turn left and at the bottom of the field go right on the path that leads along the edge of the woodland. Arriving at the metalled lane, turn left and continue past Broad House. At the end of Prince of Wales Road keep on down Back Lane to return to the Staithe Car Park.

89

WALK 16: THREE VILLAGES
The Raynhams

Start: *Helhoughton. Grid Ref: 869265.*
O.S.Map: *Landranger 132.*
Distance: *2½ or 4 miles.*
Time: *1 or 2 hours.*
Parking: *Outside Helhoughton Church.*
Refreshments: *The Greyhound, West Raynham.*

A pleasant walk through countryside and part of the Raynham Park estate. For those interested the walk encompasses two churches with a third very close by. The path is well signed by the N.C.C. green arrows.

WITH HELBOROUGH CHURCH on the left start by going past the building and turning right down Park Lane. At the end of the lane opposite Park View cottage, cross the stile on the left and turn right along by the trees. The path soon swings left towards some woods.

The nearby lake and the damp surroundings encourage luxuriant growth and on either side of the path the leaves of Butterbur, Petasites hybridus, are obvious. Petasites comes from the Greek meaning a broad-brimmed hat and John Gerard, the Elizabethan herbalist, wrote that 'the leafe is bigge and large inough to keepe a man's head from raine and from the heat of the sunne'. Powder made from the roots was once used to remove spots from the skin and the leaves were used to wrap butter.

Cross the bridge over the dyke and turn right after the kissing gate to continue along the track towards some farm buildings.
Unfortunately the lake on the right is, in summer, hidden by undergrowth. Keep on ahead through the farm and past the fine stables with stepped gable end. Bear right after the cattle grid.

To the left a view of Raynham Hall opens up through an avenue of lime trees with the lake on the right. The Hall, commenced in 1621, was built for Sir Roger Townshend and was designed by Inigo Jones. Pevsner describes it as a 'paramount house'. In the next century a descendant, Charles Townshend, was to experiment with the rotation of crops on his estate and achieved some fame for the improvement of agricultural methods.
On my last visit the attractive flint faced church was locked. The bell tower

90

and south and north porches are features of the exterior. Presumably the
latter was for the convenience of those at the Hall.

After the second cattle grid turn left up the metalled lane. (for the shorter version
of the walk turn right and rejoin the route at **) **Just short of the road (A1065) take
the 'concessionary' path on the right and follow this as far as the wartime pillbox.
Here, go right down the track which soon winds round the edge of some trees to
rejoin the N.C.C. path. Bear left to cross the bridge over the rush and willow herb
lined stream and aim for the gate ahead. Cross bridge and stile (South Raynham
church seen ahead) and turn right alongside the stream, the beginnings of the River
Wensum.**

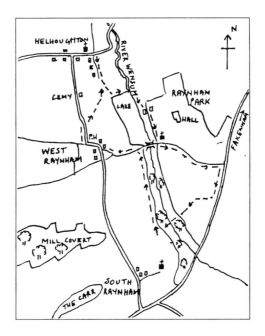

The bank of the stream is a habitat for several plants including the pale blue
flowers of water forget-me-not. Although in France the plant is called 'ne
m'oubliez pas', in this country it is Samuel Coleridge who is credited with
giving it the name in his poem 'The Keepsake'. Made into a syrup, forget-
me-nots were once used as a cure for coughs and lung complaints.

**Cross further bridges and stiles and keep on along the length of a long meadow to
a stile that gives onto the lane from West Raynham church. Bear left.**

91

** At the triangle turn right to go through the attractive village of West Raynham and after passing The Greyhound Inn bear right. In 100 metres take the path on the right diagonally across the playing field. Go between the copse and the ash tree, bear right then immediately left towards the houses ahead (do not turn right) to resume the outward path back to Helhoughton Church.

Raynham Hall

The church has an interesting history in that it was typical of many churches in the country that suffered decay during the eighteenth and nineteenth centuries. Initially larger, the tower was reduced in height and north and south aisles demolished in the 1790s. By the 1980s the church was in such a poor state that the building could not be used until extensive restoration was carried out.

The church has a special treasure in the form of a Heart Brass set in the chancel floor and there is also an unusual font. Like many paintings of the Royal Arms, Helhoughton's, painted for James II, had to be up-dated for the union with Scotland in 1705.

WALK 17: CASTLE, MILL AND PRIORY
Castle Acre and the River Nar

Start: *Castle Acre. Grid Ref: 816151.*
O.S.Map: *Landranger 132.*
Distance: *6 miles.*
Time: *2½ hours.*
Parking: *Near the Village Post Office.*
Refreshments: *Two Inns and Tea Rooms.*

> *An attractive square, an imposing gateway, castle ruins with impressive ramparts, a very welcoming church and a Cluniac priory claimed to be the best in southern England all make this village worth exploring. The walk takes in all this and in addition there is a lovely outward stretch along the River Nar and through woods.*

FROM THE POST OFFICE go past the church along Priory Road. Turn right at the end (or left if visiting the Priory, see below) and then left down the gravel track. Just past the 'S' bend take the path on the left which runs alongside the River Nar.

Later a gate gives into woodland. Keep ahead where a track crosses to arrive, after an open space, at a bridge over the stream. The path goes between fences with Mill House on the left, over a slightly longer bridge to the road. Here turn left and at the next junction go straight ahead keeping West Acre Church on the right. In a short while take the second of the two footpaths on the left and follow the hedge of hawthorn, oak and ash trees. Where the path curves right go left soon to pass a small copse on the left. Keep forward at the first crossing of tracks and at the next crossing turn left. After passing under the power lines keep straight ahead to turn right on arriving at a lane.
Go past a moat on the left - an attraction for herons (was it only a fishpond for the Priory?) and bear left to the ford.

> From here to the village the route follows Peddars Way.

After the ford take the first turning right (Blind Lane), turn left at the road and then right down Cuckstool Lane. A path at the end leads up to the ramparts of the castle. Go round the castle and follow the Nar Valley Way sign to return to the village.

> The village stands in what was once the outer bailey of the castle and the thirteenth century gateway at the east end of the village is the only building to remain intact. The castle earthworks are, however, very impressive and

the scale of the castle befitted the status of its builder, William de Warenne, who was William the Conqueror's son-in-law. The walled village was built between the castle and the priory, the latter being founded by de Warenne in 1090 after his visit to the abbey of Cluny in France.

The ruins of the priory are thought by some to be the finest in southern England and the west front of the priory church is certainly impressive. The gatehouse seen from the priory road is a later addition of the sixteenth century and was where the steward would meet people from the world outside to discuss business.

Although there were only 30 monks the priory became wealthy possibly because it lay on the pilgrim route to Little Walsingham. It is open daily except for Monday and Tuesday from November to March.

The village church of St James the Great is an inspiring place and has a fifteenth century painted screen and pulpit. An exceptionally tall font cover dates from the same period.

The village declined after the dissolution and later became part of the Holkham estate. It still had a number of industries in Victorian times including a foundry, a tannery, a brick kiln, two mills and two blacksmiths.

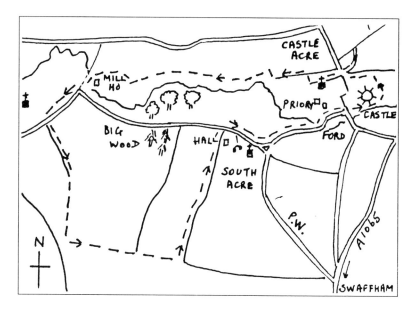

WALK 18: BETWEEN TWO VILLAGES
North and South Creake

Start: *North Creake. Grid Ref: 854378.*
O.S.Map: *Landranger 132.*
Distance: *9 miles.*
Time: *3½ hours.*
Parking: *Opposite North Creake Church.*
Refreshments: *The Ostrich Inn or packed lunch.*

> *This is a walk - perhaps tramp would be a better word - to keep for a cool day in summer or a bracing winter's day when the distant views across open countryside are clear cut and when a sharper pace is easier. The walk, which circles the watershed of the River Burn, gives a good impression of this part of Norfolk. The river flows through the two villages except in very dry summers.*

FROM THE CHURCH go towards the village and almost immediately turn left to find the path behind the village hall. (In the summer a path is left through the crops.) Follow the curve round to the right to meet a gravel track and here turn left. Continue ahead past the farm on the right (Ringate Farm) on to a grassy path and later gravel and grass. This stretch goes well past Sly's Barn seen on the ridge to the left. On arriving at a lane and a pond on the right turn left up the rise. Shammer House may be seen behind. Where tracks cross keep ahead (hedge on both sides), straight on at the next crossing and soon, where the track forks, bear left. (The corner is marked by four or more oaks in the hedge.)

Follow this track for nearly two miles and at the road turn left to go past Bluestone Farm.

> In the other direction the road rises to Bloodgate Hill thought to be the site of a battle with the Danes. (This is depicted on the village sign.) There are the remains of a fort half a mile up the road which, it is thought, was once three times larger than the one at Warham (see Walk 6) but much has been destroyed by ploughing.
> South Creake Church is worth a visit to see the very fine rood screen.

At the war memorial follow the Fakenham sign past the three-storeyed malt house and the village sign and take the path left at the side of the Ostrich Inn. This becomes a grassy track with a mixed hedge of oak, ash and hawthorn, somewhat older than those on the first part of the walk. After a mile Whin Close Villa is reached. Keep forward and turn left on to a stretch of the Roman road that extends

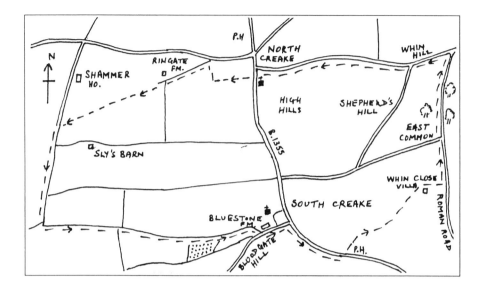

from Toftrees to Holkham. Continue on ahead at the crossroads through East Common woods as far as the bend. Turn left down the lane s.p. North and South Creake.
In the summer wild roses adorn the hedge all the way back to North Creake.

The Dog Rose, a name given to it by the Romans (Rosa Canina) flowers in June and July and the resulting hips, rich in Vitamin C, are used to make rose hip syrup.

'Unkempt about those hedges blows
An English unofficial rose.' (Rupert Brooke)

WALK 19: ACROSS COMMON AND BY RIVER
Narborough

Start: *Narborough. Grid Ref: 747129.*
O.S.Map: *Landranger 132.*
Distance: *5 miles.*
Time: *2½ hours.*
Parking: *Room for one car outside church.*
Refreshments: *Packed lunch.*

A pleasant walk across Narborough Common (now farmland), through the dense Marham Fen and returning along the bank of the River Nar. If time does not allow for the whole walk, a stroll along the river bank is well worthwhile. The Nar Valley Way may be found about 100 metres on the left past the church at the end of a short cul-de-sac of houses.

TAKE THE PATH between walls beside the church. After the last bungalow follow the path diagonally across the field. At the lane turn right down a gravel track and where it bends to the right go diagonally across the field. Continue on ahead at the belt of trees and also later at the crossing of tracks, keeping the hedge on your left. Where the track curves to the right keep forward and, going to the left of a telegraph pole, cross the ditch and the next field (path left through any crop) towards the trees.

Go straight over the gravel track. At the next track turn left and in 80 metres turn right down a sandy path into Marham Fen.

The Wildlife Trust is co-operating with Anglian Water Authority who have a large water abstraction station at Marham Fen. The fen has been allowed to dry out and, being unmanaged, trees have gradually encroached on the grassland. Now ponds are being excavated and hawthorn and birch scrub is being removed from grassland thus allowing flowers such as the bee and twayblade orchid to regenerate.

Keep ahead on this path until arriving at a gate adjacent to Anglian Water Authority premises. Here turn right to re-enter the wood. Emerging from the wood, cross the gravel track and follow the telegraph poles towards the sluice on the river. Bear right and at the bridge negotiate the metal gate and continue along the path on the right side of the river.

During the summer swallows and martins hawk the river for insects and occasionally duck and coot scuttle for cover as you pass.

Martins can be readily distinguished from swallows by their white rump which contrasts with the rest of their black appearance. Their tails are less deeply forked than the swallow's and, except for the juveniles, the latter have long streamers to their tails.

Remains of an iron water wheel, festooned with wild rose, and brick plinths are signs of the past history of the river.

At the end of the path turn right out of the cul-de-sac to return to the church.

The village of Narborough has a long and interesting history. Traces of Bronze, Iron and Roman occupation have been found in the area and by 1086 the Domesday recorded 'Nereburgh' as having 41 working men. The coming of the railway in 1846 was met with great opposition as was its closure in 1968 and, up until the middle of this century, the River Nar was a busy thoroughfare of trade from Kings Lynn. In World War I the village boasted the largest aerodrome in Britain. Much of the old village was demolished in the 1950s along with an old tithe barn and eighteenth century almshouses.

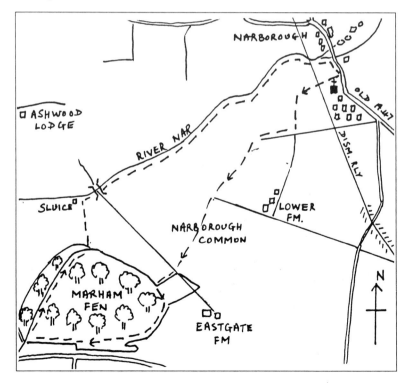

98

WALK 20: A HISTORIAN'S TRAIL
Mileham to Whissonsett

Start: *Mileham Grid Ref: 917195.*
O.S.Map: *Landranger 132.*
Distance: *6 or 8 miles.*
Time: *3½ hours.*
Parking: *Between village sign and post office.*
Refreshments: *The Swan, Whissonsett.*

A tramp across fields, first to visit Tittleshall Church with its memorials and then to the deserted village of Godwick and on to Whissonsett. The return to Mileham is by lanes or, for the adventurous, across poorly signed field paths. A linear walk to Godwick and return the same way is a shorter alternative.

It will be seen that the village of Mileham lives up to its name! It also has a long history since Roman artifacts have been discovered near the village including a silver dish now in the British Museum. The Normans also built a castle here but only small remains are visible now.

WALK TOWARDS THE POST OFFICE and turn right down Back Lane. After the last house turn right down a gravel track by The Old Sawmill. Just before the track curves right go over the wooden bridge on the left and diagonally across the field to a 'covered barbed wire' crossing. Negotiate this and a similar one opposite and continue on a diagonal line towards trees to follow the edge of the wood.
At the corner of the wood bear left and then right and keep on the diagonal line aiming for pylons on the horizon. Meeting a ditch follow this to a plank bridge, cross and turn right. At the lane and Cokesford Cottage turn left and by the junction to Tittleshall House Farm take the footpath on the right towards the church. The path leads to a gate in the corner of the field and then forward to the lane on the left.

The lane soon leads to St Mary's Church which contains several memorials to the Coke family beginning with the tomb of Sir Edward Coke (1552-1634) who lived at Godwick Hall (see below) and was Attorney General during the reigns of Queen Elizabeth I and James I. There is an alabaster monument to his wife, Bridget, and other relatives are remembered including a magnificent monument to a famous descendant, Thomas William Coke, Earl of Leicester, the agriculturist (see page 35).

Continue past the church and at the end of Church Lane bear right and take

the second footpath on the right opposite Manor House Farm pond. Follow the hedge round the field skirting a copse surrounding a moat on the right. At the end of the second field follow the path diagonally over the next field aiming to the left of the church tower seen ahead. Go across the field keeping the church tower and later a barn on the right towards a stile and a notice about Godwick.

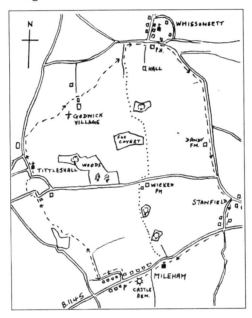

Godwick is one of nineteen sites of deserted villages in Norfolk. The site is open to view between the months of April and September although it is possible to gain some impression from the footpath. The village developed on a boulder clay plateau which may well have become too wet to be farmed. It was probably in decline when Sir Edward Coke built his house and was finally deserted around 1630 when it was merged with the parish of Tittleshall. The manor house was demolished after World War II. The shallow depression or hollow way running parallel to the hedge marks the street through the village. Tracks run from the street away to the right. The pond in the centre of the hollow way is of a later date and possibly formed as a result of clay digging.

The barn, built of rubbed red brick dates from the seventeenth century when the village was enclosed, probably for sheep. (An aerial photograph of the site is to be found in Richard Muir's book)

There is still a flock of sheep in the adjoining field. I wonder whether sheep have been farmed there continuously for the last three hundred years?

Godwick deserted village

The return to Mileham may be made by retracing steps along the outward path. An alternative is to continue the circular walk to Whissonsett and return by road through Stansfield (4½ miles) or by poorly signed paths across fields (3½ miles).

To continue to Whissonsett bear left after the stile and immediately right through a metal gate at the side of the farm. Follow the hedge round for about 200 metres to a gap and here turn right on a path which crosses fields (possibly through crops) to meet a yellow waymark sign, the first of three, leading to a plank bridge. Cross and go diagonally over the field using the power lines as a guide. After passing under the power lines it's decision time! **Turn left down the track for Whissonsett or right for the poorly marked path to Mileham.

A turn left to the lane into Whissonsett may be preferred and the return walk to Mileham can be made along the road turning right after The Swan public house (s.p. Stansfield) and in two miles bearing right to Mileham.

For the return by field turn right at the point starred ** and proceed to the point where the hedge veers right. Keep forward aiming for the right edge of the wood ahead. Go round the back of the wood and across the meadow aiming for the left edge of the wood on the right. Turn along the left edge of the wood and keep ahead across fields to a lane. Here turn right past Wicken Farm and in a few metres turn left at the side of a pond partially hidden by a hedge. Keep forward, proceeding along the right edge of a wood ahead and also a second wood further on. Continue in the same direction to meet the road and turn right back into Mileham.

WALK 21: BY CUT AND OUSE
The Wiggenhalls

Start: *Wiggenhall St Mary Magdalen. Grid Ref: 598114.*
O.S.Map: *Landranger 143.*
Distance: *6½ miles.*
Time: *3½ hours.*
Parking: *Near the church.*
Refreshments: *Crown & Anchor, Wiggenhall St Mary the Virgin;*
The Cock, Wiggenhall St Mary Magdalen.

To anyone not familiar with the marsh fenland south of the Wash this makes an interesting walk across farmland to the Middle Level and returning along the banks of the River Ouse and the Cut-Off channel.

FROM ST MARY MAGDALEN CHURCH walk towards the telephone box to turn right at the junction. In a few metres turn left by the side of Church Farm House and opposite 4, Lynn Road. (The footpath sign may be obscured by undergrowth.) At the end of the ditch turn right and in 20 metres left to continue in the same direction beside a 'nissen type' animal shelter. Proceed to the end of the ditch and then cut straight across the field to the lane.
Here turn right towards a pair of houses. The lane devolves into a track bearing left then right beside a dyke. A grassy track eventually divides after half a mile, so here veer left alongside the hedge with a ditch on the right. At the road turn left across the bridge over the Middle Level and in about 100 metres go right down the lane. In about half a mile go right again at the next lane. Just short of the bridge cross the stile on the left and continue forward along the grassy bank of the Level. Keep forward crossing another stile to reach the bridge by the Middle Level Pumping Station. Turn right for Wiggenhall St Germans.

In 1953 there was severe flooding in the area when the River Ouse was breached. To prevent a repetition a new channel, the Middle Level, was cut as far as Bedford. The pumping station, built in the 1930s and now electrified, controls the flow of water allowing it out to sea via the Ouse.

Follow the road round passing the bridge over the old sluice opened in 1877 bearing right then left through the village to pass over the Ouse bridge. Turn right beside the Crown and Anchor pub and ascend the bank just before the gate to the church.

The path runs along the bank past the sad ruin of St Peter's Church

The ruined church of Wiggenhall St Peter.

perched high with a view over the surrounding country, a flat landscape of reclaimed marsh, low trees, telegraph poles and squat houses relieved in height only by church towers and the occasional group of lombardy poplars.

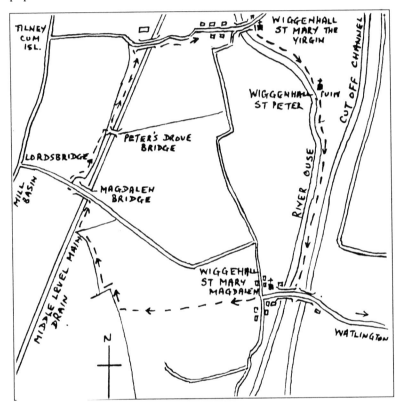

Soon the path meets the juncture of the Ouse and the Relief Channel - a point at which the three Wiggenhall churches can be seen. Continue forward as far as the gates and the road. Turn right to return to the start point.

A great feature of the church here is the medieval stained glass dating from about 1450 in the north aisle windows. In five windows there are tiny depictions of over forty saints, many of whom will be new names to most people. They are listed in the church guide.

WALK 22: A TWELFTH CENTURY VILLAGE
Castle Rising

Start: *Castle Rising Church. Grid Ref: 666248.*
O.S.Map: *Landranger 132.*
Distance: *3½ miles.*
Time: *1½ hours.*
Parking: *East or West of the church.*
Refreshments: *The Black Horse, Castle Rising.*

> *A delightful walk through this very attractive village circling through the surrounding fields to follow a short stretch of the River Babingley and returning through a beautiful wood.*

IF PARKING BETWEEN the church and Trinity Hospice walk up to go past the Black Horse and turn right to go past the church lych gate and the war memorial. Turn right at the bottom of the lane and in 50 metres bear left. Where the track bends to the left turn right and at the metalled lane bear left.
Across the fields to the left are the banks of the River Babingley which swings round to meet the lane further on. Keep forward to take the footpath on the right beside the river bridge. Follow the stream to the road, the A149.

> In spring and summer the banks of the stream are covered with a variety of wild flowers which provide an interesting diversion. Water forget-me-not, valerian, knapweed and meadowsweet are just a few. Meadowsweet, often found in wet meadows, has upright clusters of fragrant, creamy white flowers hence its name. The plant was much favoured in Tudor times for spreading on the floors of houses to mask unwanted smells. It was once called 'medesweete' since it was used to flavour mead. It flowers from June to September.

Wait for a gap in the traffic in both directions and cross with great care - the road may be busy especially during the summer months.
Cross the stile opposite and follow the river for a short way before crossing the meadow to a gate seen in the right hand corner. Keep on ahead on the lane to the edge of the wood - Fowler's Plantation - and take the footpath ahead which leads through the wood for half a mile to gain the road. (A footpath on the right leads back to the village to shorten the walk if necessary.) At the road turn right and after crossing the A149, keep forward to return to the village.

> The castle dates from the middle of the twelfth century and was built by William de Albini who was also responsible for the castle at New

Buckenham (see Walk 1). The keep is one of the largest in England and is similar to the one at Norwich with its decorated arches.
St Lawrence Church near the start of the walk has a fine Norman west front and doorway. On the other side of the church is the Trinity Hospice founded in 1609 by Henry Howard. It is now an almshouse for ladies who may be seen on Sundays at church wearing their red cloaks adorned with the badge of the Howard family.

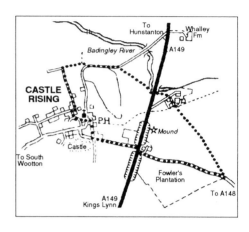

St Lawrence Church, Castle Rising.

WALK 23: BY RIVER AND RAIL
Marsham to Buxton

Start: *Marsham. Grid Ref: 197241.*
O.S.Map: *Landranger 133.*
Distance: *7 miles.*
Time: *3 hours.*
Parking: *Old Norwich Road (adjacent to A140).*
Refreshments: *Black Lion, Buxton or packed lunch by the rivr.*

A varied and most interesting walk along the bank of the River Bure and the Bure Valley Railway, returning across parkland and field paths. The first part of the walk can be rather muddy especially after wet weather or during the winter so boots may be desirable.

START BY CROSSING the A140 near the bus shelter and go down the path called Rodgate. The path soon emerges onto a wide stretch of grazing pasture and to avoid the ditches it is probably best to keep close to the hedge on the right. Follow this to the corner of the field marked by several ash trees and then turn left along the hedge. Follow this hedge for some way negotiating ditches when necessary to a stile (signed by a yellow waymark).

Soon the course of the Mermaid stream becomes obvious and this may be followed to the road which is gained by a gate near the hedge on the right. (Don't cross over the stream by the small brick bridge).

At the road turn left and in 20 metres take the footpath on the right. Ahead, after a stile, is the railway bridge. Continue along by the stream under the bridge as far as a gate seen to the right.

(It is possible to mount the embankment on the far side of the bridge and continue along the line to Buxton. This shortens the walk by about ¾ of a mile but misses out the attractive section along the River Bure.)

Then turn left on the path, over one plank bridge and keep ahead with the stream on the left to the steps of a longer bridge. This crosses the Bure and allows access to the church at Burgh-next-Aylsham.

For those interested in architecture, this small church of St Mary's is well worth a visit since the chancel is a beautiful example of the Early English style. It was highly praised by Sir Gilbert Scott, the architect, who saw it as one of the few examples of the transitional stage between the Norman and Early English periods. The church tower and the seven sacrament font are also of interest.

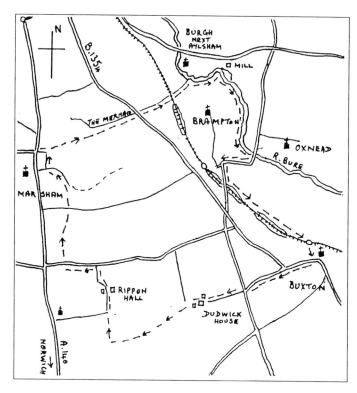

The path continues to the right just before the bridge along the edge of the river. After passing the Mill and sluice, negotiate the gate to continue along the bank of the river. The mill stream of the river rejoins a little further on and the path then winds between trees. Keep on ahead by the river until reaching the road which goes right towards the village of Brampton. Here bear left to the railway bridge and the steps up to the embankment. Turn left at the top and go forward as far as the halt at Buxton. Cross the line before the station, bear left through the estate and at the road turn right away from the church towards the Crown Inn.

Veer left down Crown Road as far as the Black Lion crossing Brook Street to continue down the parkland drive to Dudwick House. Go straight on between the House and Dudwick Cottage, past the metal farm gate and up the rise. At the cross tracks keep straight on to turn right at the next track just short of a wood.

The path then cuts between the buildings of Rippon Farm. Turn left at the lane beyond the farm and about ¼ mile before the A140 follow the well-maintained footpath on the right. Cross straight over the next lane, bearing left at the sandy track, then right to return to the Rodgate and Marsham.

WALK 24: TWO VILLAGE CHURCHES
Trunch to Knapton

Start: *Trunch. Grid Ref: 287348.*
O.S.Map: *Landranger 133.*
Distance: *4¼ miles.*
Time: *1¾ hours.*
Parking: *Trunch Social Club Car Park.*
Refreshments: *The Crown, Trunch.*

> *This walk traverses the road between the two villages returning by way of field paths. It provides an opportunity to appreciate the glories of the two churches each with their own treasures.*

FROM TRUNCH CHURCH walk past the Crown public house and turn right at the junction (s.p. Knapton). At the crossroads in Knapton continue ahead down The Street (s.p. Paston) past Knapton Hall to the church of St Peter and St Paul.

The double hammer-beam roof, said to be one of the finest in East Anglia, was erected in 1503. There are eleven bays with two tiers of figures depicting prophets, apostles and angels - all the Company of Heaven. Underneath is a more modern addition - a row of angels with wings outspread lean out over the nave. There is a tradition that the roof was not designed for Knapton but was acquired from a storm-wrecked ship en route elsewhere. Alternatively, it may have been made locally from the wreckage of the ships.
The thirteenth century font with its cover dating from the reign of Queen Anne is also of interest.

On leaving the church turn left and, in 50 metres, the walk continues down Timber Loke soon bearing left to the embankment of the dismantled railway from Mundesley to North Walsham.
Go over the bridge with its steel arch to the corner of the field and turn right down a hedge-lined path. After half a mile look for a gap in the hedge on the right and a finger-post indicating a path across the field towards a house. (Should the path be completely blocked by a crop continue to a lane. Turn right and then right again to regain the route at the reserve.) Aim for the left of the house where the path meets a fence. At the road turn right.

Opposite is the Knapton Cutting Nature Reserve, part of the Paston Way between North Walsham and Mundesley, which is a haven for several varieties of butterflies, 'best seen on a calm sunny day in the summer'.

In 20 metres take the path on the left and at the bottom of the field bear left on the other side of the hedge to follow this round the field. At the corner, veer obliquely right and follow the path to the road. Trunch Church can be seen ahead. Bear right at the road and just past The Old Coach House, go down the path on the left veering to the right at the fork. Continue ahead as far as the hedge on the right and follow this to the road to return to Trunch.

Before leaving the village a visit to the church is worthwhile. The octagonal font, one of only four in the country, has an unusual and beautifully carved oak cover which is supported on six legs. It rises high above the font to a hexagonal panelled top which would have originally been painted. It probably suffered defacement in the seventeenth century as did the Rood screen.

A memorial in the chancel to Philip Ward links the church to Burnham Thorpe (Walk 4) for he married Horatia, the daughter of Lord Nelson and Lady Hamilton.

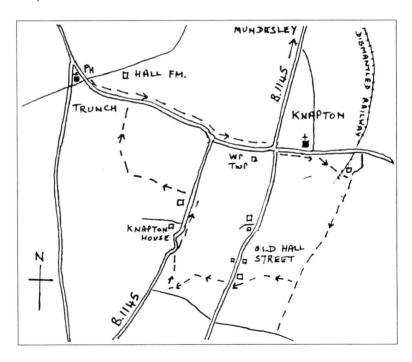

WALK 25: FOREST AND FLINT
Weeting to Grimes Graves

Start: *Weeting Church. Grid Ref: 777893*
O.S.Map: *Landranger 144.*
Distance: *7 miles.*
Time: *3 hours.*
Parking: *Near Weeting Church.*
Refreshments: *Drinks available at Grimes Graves.*

Another visit to Breckland. The route goes through an attractive mixed wood and across heathland to Grimes Graves and returns along the forest trails. The remains of Weeting Castle are near the start and Thetford Forest Visitor Centre ia not far away on the B1106 to Brandon. Visiting times for Grimes Graves are listed at the end of the walk.

There was an Anglo-Saxon settlement at Weeting. Domesday Book has an entry for Wetynge, the name deriving from a Saxon word meaning Wet Fields. Also Weeting's proximity to Grimes Graves may well have meant that it was inhabited 2,500 years earlier.

STARTING FROM THE CHURCH follow the track north past the church tower and through the nearby farmyard of Home Farm. Continue ahead towards a house set in the trees. After passing an open space the track forks. Here, turn right and then left along a straight track bordered by trees on the left. The pine forest, edged by beeches, soon changes to a mixed wood.

This stretch of forest path is a good environment for butterflies. Even in late autumn the clear yellow Brimstone may be seen fluttering through the trees.

Turn right on arriving at the A1065 and take the next turning on the left s.p. West Tofts. (There's bags of roadside space for walking!) Go forward along this road and after passing some white metal gates on the right, look out for a gap in the fence bordering an Army training area. Here, turn right on to the signed footpath which passes between trees to emerge on to open heath. The path is indistinct across this rough ground so aim for a small copse of pine trees immediately ahead and, on breasting the rise, the car park and the solitary building at Grimes Graves come into view. The fence may be crossed near the copse.

Visitors to the site are, after donning a hard hat, able to descend the one

111

shaft that has been opened up to the public, Pit No 1. Access to the 30 ft shaft and its seven galleries is by ladder.
433 shafts have now been surveyed by archaeologists. Most of the deep pits lie to the east and south of the visitor centre. Aerial photographs of the area show the infilled shafts to resemble a mass of bomb craters.

After visiting the site of the mines, either retrace your steps across the heath back to the road (Point 'A') or if preferred, follow the route for cars which crosses the cattle grid and leads back to the road, and then turn left to reach Point 'A'. From here return to the white gates passed earlier and turn left on to the forest ride which leaves the road at right angles and is marked by a black and yellow pole. Keep on in this direction ignoring crossing tracks until reaching a point crossed by a red sandy track. An oak tree on the corner is marked by the number 15.
Turn right here and continue on this track to return to the A1065. Cross straight over to continue on the footpath leading into Emily's Wood and to Brickkiln Farm. At the farm the path veers to the left of some majestic beech trees. In 100 metres or so turn right and continue ahead to regain the outward path within sight of a farm cottage. Turn left to return to Weeting Church.

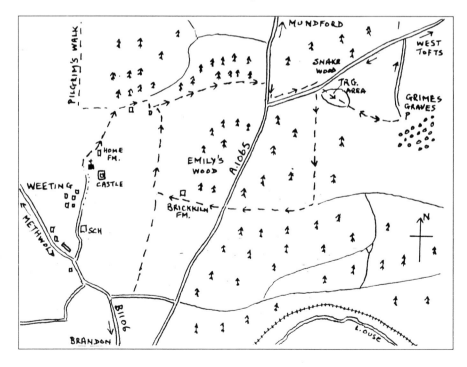

The ruins of Weeting Castle lie 100 metres to the east of the church. The castle was really a large fortified house surrounded by a moat. It was built in early medieval times about 1180 and consisted of a large aisled hall with wings of three storeys.

Grimes Graves is open to visitors April to September from 10 until 6 and October from 10 until 6 or dusk (closed 1 - 2).
Winter months open 10 until 4 except Monday and Tuesday.

Grimes Graves

List of Trees and Shrubs for hedge dating

Alder	Elm: Wych, English, etc.	Poplar: Aspen, Black,White
Apple	Furze	Privet (wild)
Ash	Guelder-rose	Rowan
Beech	Hawthorn: hedgerow, woodland	
Blackthorn	Hazel	Sallow
Briar	Holly	Service
Broom	Hornbeam	Spindle
Buckthorn	Lime: ordinary, pry	Sycamore
Cherry	Maple	Wayfaring tree
Cherry-plum	Oak: pedunculate, sessile	Whitebeam
Dogwood	Pine	Willow: crack, white
Elder	Plum	Yew

The Greenway,
Little Walsingham.
(see Walk 7)

Nature Reserves in Norfolk

Key : **NWT** *Norfolk Wildlife Trust.*
01603 625540
NT *National Trust.*
RSPB *Royal Society for the Protection of Birds. 01603 661662*
EN *English Nature.*
NNR *National Nature Reserve.*

North Norfolk Coast Area

OS 133	**Blakeney Point**	TG 048453	Terns, Geese, Waders, Seals.	NT
OS 133	**Cley Marshes**	TG 054441	Various bird life Avocet, Bittern. Closed Mondays. Permit.	NWT
OS 132	**East Winch Common**	TF 698160	Heath, Woodland, Boggy plants. Tits, Warblers.	NWT
OS 133	**Foxley Wood N.R.**	TG 049229	Ancient wood. Spring Flowers, Fungi, Butterflies, Woodpeckers.	NWT
OS 132	**Holkham N.N.R.**	TF 845443 TF 914454	Various birds, dunes, Pines, red squirrels.	EN

Access from Overy Staithe by seawall or by beach at Wells.

OS 133	**Holt Lowes**	TG 082376	Bog. Heath. Mire. Dragonflies.	NWT
OS 132	**Holme Dunes**	TF 697438	Birds, Natterjack Toads. Permit.	NWT
OS 133	**Morston & Stiffkey**	TG 005443	Various birds, Saltmarsh plants.	NT
OS 133	**Salthouse Marsh**	TG 082443	Migratory birds.	NWT
OS 132	**Scolt Head Island** Access by boat Info. 01485 210719	TG 465810	Migratory birds.	NWT
OS 132	**Snettisham N.R.** Info. 01603 661662	TF 646335	Various birds.	RSPB
OS 132	**Thursford Wood**	TF 97933	Ancient wood, Fungi, lichens.	NWT
OS 132	**Titchwell Marsh N.R.** (01485 210432)	TF 751448	Reclaimed Marsh, Various Birds, incl. marsh harrier, bittern.	RSPB

West Norfolk

OS 132	Narborough Railway Line	TF 750118	Chalkland flowers.	NWT
OS 132	Ringstead Downs	TF 705400	Chalkland flowers, Butterflies.	NWT
OS 132	Roydon Common	TF 698228	Wetland plants, dragonflies.	NWT
OS 132	Syderstone Common	TF 835316	Heath. Natterjack Toads.	NWT

Central Norfolk

OS 144	Ashwellthorpe Wood	TM 140980	Ancient Wood. Spring Flowers, Hornbeam Coppice	NWT
OS 133	Booton Common	TG 112228	Fen. Orchids, etc.	NWT
OS 134	Hethel Old Thorn	TG 171005	Ancient hawthorn. Nearby churchyard.	NWT
OS 132	Hoe Rough	TF 978168	Meadow Flowers.	NWT
OS 132	Honeypot Wood	TF 932142	Ancient coppiced wood. Woodland plants & birds.	NWT
OS 133	Sparham Pools	TF 073178	Gravel Pits. Various birds.	NWT
OS 144	Wayland Wood	TL 924995	Ancient managed woodland spring/summer flowers.	NWT

Breckland

OS 144	East Wretham Heath	TL 913887	Breckland Heath. Meres, various pants. Birds.	NWT
OS 144	New Buckenham Common	TM 095906	Grassland.Various flowers, orchids.	NWT
OS 144	Thompson Common	TL 934967	Grassland, Woods. Pingos, Various plants. Butterflies.	NWT
OS 143 /OS144	Weeting Heath Open Apr. to Aug.	TL 756881	Breckland Heath. Stone Curlew. permits (01842 827615)	NNR

Broadland

OS 134	Alderfen Broad	TG 355195	Wildfowl, Dragonflies.	NWT
OS 134	Berney Marshes	TG 460050	Waders, wildfowl.	RSPB
OS 134	Breydon Water N.R.	TG 495070	Waders, wildfowl.	RSPB
OS 134	Cockshoot Broad	TG 343163	Reclaimed broad. Various birds. Butterflies.	NWT

Broadland (cont.)

OS 134	Horsey Mere	TG 456223	Various birds, plants.	NT
OS 134	Hickling Broad	TG 428222	Various plants,birds,insects	NWT
	(01692 598276) Book for boat to hides.			
OS 134	Martham Broad	TG466203	Harrier, bearded tits, butterflies.	NWT
OS 134	Strumpshaw Fen	TG 344065	Reed & sedge beds. Wild flower walk.	RSPB
OS 134	Surlingham Church Marsh	TG 306064	Various birds.	RSPB
OS 134	Upton Fen	TG 381138	Fenland Plants. Dragonflies.	NWT

Thompson Common

How to read a Grid Reference

TO HELP PINPOINT a place on the ground all Ordnance Survey maps are divided into small squares by vertical and horizontal Grid lines. These lines are numbered. All references are given as six figured numbers and the first three refer to the number of the vertical lines or Eastings and the last three refer to the horizontal lines or Northings.

Take the point on the sample map of Bircham Newton Church.

First quote the Eastings.

Find the first vertical line to the left of the church and read the figures at the end of the line at the top or bottom of the map, in this case - 76
Estimate in tenths of a square from the grid line to the church, i.e. 9

Then quote the Northings.

Find the first horizontal line below the church and read the figures at the end of the line at the right or left margin of the map, in this case - 33
Estimate in tenths of a square from the grid line to the church, i.e. 9

The sample reference is therefore 769339

Following the same method give grid references for Pond Farm, the tumulus, and for Great Bircham Windmill.

Pond Farm   777328   Tumulus   775316   Bircham Windmill   761327
Note that Great Bircham Church will be 770326.

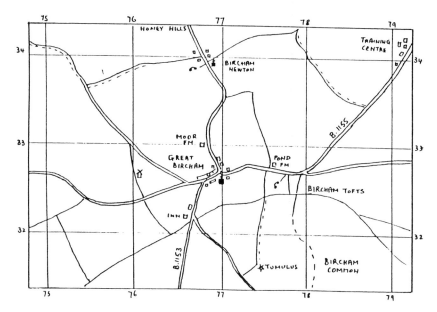

118

About the Author

JOHN PARDY moved to Suffolk 28 years ago with his wife Vivien and daughter Jess. Their first home was a coastguard cottage on the beach at Shingle Street. The Suffolk coast, its wildlife and history inspired an interest in walking and the discovery of places only accessible on foot. Following early retirement from his job as Headteacher of a Primary School, John now has time to record his walks and develop his other interests in music, birdwatching and gardening. Now living in a small village on the Felixstowe peninsula, he is considered an authority on walking in Suffolk and shares his walks with friends in the area and also his dog, Ben.
This book is a follow-up to John's 'A Walkers' Guide to Suffolk'.

Bibliography

Ager, D.V.	Introducing Geology	Faber 1961
Bartlett, D.	Discovering North Norfolk and the Broads	Leading Edge 1993
Clarke P & M	Where to watch Birds in East Anglia	A & C Black 1995
Dymond, D	The Norfolk Landscape	Alastair Press 1990
Harrod W.	The Norfolk Guide	Alastair Press 1988
Knox M.	Norfolk	Shire Publications 1994
Jebb M.	East Anglian Anthology	National Trust 1980
Mason & McClelland	Background to Breckland	Providence Press 1994
Parker & Dye	The Fenland	David & Charles 1976
Pevsner	The Buildings of Norfolk	Harmondsworth 1962
Pocock T.	Norfolk	Pimlico 1995
Rackham O.	A History of the Countryside	Weidenfeld 1995
Ravensdale & Muir	East Anglian Landscape	M.Joseph 1984
Reed M.	The Landscape of Britain	Routledge 1990
Sager P.	East Anglia	Pallas Athene 1990
Seymour J.	Guide to East Anglia	Collins 1988
Timpson J.	Timpson's Travels in East Anglia	Heinneman 1990
Wade-Martins P.	Historical Atlas of Norfolk	Norfolk Museum 1992
Wade-Martins S.A.	History of Norfolk	Chichester 1984
W.I.	The Norfolk Village Book	Countryside Books 1994
Readers Digest	WildFlowers of Britain	Readers Digest 1989

A whispering and watery Norfolk sound
Telling of all the moonlit reeds around.

from 'The Bure'. John Betjeman.

To see a world in a grain of sand.

'Auguries of Innocence'. William Blake.